VALLEY OF FAITH

THOMAS ARIAZ

Valley of Faith

Copyright © 2021 by *Thomas Ariaz*

All rights reserved. No part of this publication may be reproduced, distributed, or transmitted in any form or by any means, including photocopying, recording, or other electronic or mechanical methods, without the prior written permission of the author, except in the case of brief quotations embodied in critical reviews and certain other non-commercial uses permitted by copyright law.

ISBN
978-1-954932-84-5 (Paperback)
978-1-954932-83-8 (eBook)

*Dedicated To and In Memory of My Beloved Son
Thomas Andrew Ariaz.
May He Rest In Peace and In Everlasting Life.*

A LETTER TO GOD

Joey walked along the railroad tracks heading home from school. It was a cold day in December. As he kicked an empty can, he thought about his grandpa. His grandpa Simon hadn't been feeling well. He seemed to be running out of energy more often and he slept a lot.

Although he was now sixty-eight years old and retired from the railroad, Simon Guerra had always been an energetic man and never seemed to be idle. Now he had taken over raising little Joseph, who was nicknamed Joey, after Joey's parents, his son Richard and his wife Amy, had died in a car accident when Joey was only a year old. Now eight, Joey didn't remember anything about his parents. His grandpa Simon was the only parent he knew. His grandma Maria, Simon's wife, had passed away before Joey was born, and so he never got to know her. Now Simon had grown to be very bitter about his losses.

Simon's house, located at the edge of town, is old and small but Simon has maintained it well. With its two bedrooms and one bath, it's spacious and comfortable enough for himself and Joey.

Minnie, Simon's sister who lives next door, knows how Simon has changed over the past few years. When Joey's parents died, she had offered to help Simon with Joey, but he had told her that he could raise Joey himself. He did not even allow Minnie to take Joey to Mass. Since then, he had never asked her or anyone else for any help.

Joey stopped at the corner store just two blocks from his school. He walked in and headed straight for the freezer where the ice cream was kept. He slid open one of the glass covers and reached in for his favorite snack, an ice cream sandwich, even if it was cold day. He took it out and placed it on the counter as he reached inside his pocket for some change to pay for it. Julio, the store owner, came over to where Joey was standing on the other side of the counter. He always spoke to Joey with kindness, "Hey, little man. How's your grandpa?" Joey looked at Julio, and just shrugged his shoulders.

Joey was not a shy boy, but when talking with people he usually didn't say much. It was probably because he was used to his grandfather not a being a socializing or associating person with anyone and he didn't have any close friends. That seemed to affect Joey's personality in some ways.

Simon is known to everyone in the neighborhood. They know of Simon's family losses and his bitterness over the losses. People say that Simon has changed and that he isn't well. A devout Catholic in the past, he had always attended Mass with his wife and family and helped the church whenever it was needed. But now, he would not even go near the church and he has often said things that many thought he did not mean. Not even Father John, the pastor at St. Lucy's Catholic Church, could reach out or talk to him.

After his son's and daughter-in-law's burial, Simon had gone straight home with Joey in his arms. No one saw him for more than a month after that. Since then, he was somewhat of a recluse and only went outside of his property when he needed to go to the store or pay his bills.

Minnie had tried to talk to Simon, but he would just sit and stare into space. When he did say anything, it was with bitterness and disdain for the church. It was no secret that he had blamed God for his misfortune. In the past, Minnie had heard him talk out loud when he drank too much about how devoted he had been to God, but that now He had let him down and had "turned His back" on him.

Joey was walking in the neighborhood now, but when he got near his house he saw an ambulance parked in front with its red lights flashing. Joey's heart started to beat fast. He ran to the house. His aunt Minnie was on the porch. She grabbed him before he could dash into the house.

"Joey," she said to him. "Your grandpa is sick and he needs to go to the hospital. Don't worry, *mijo*. He'll be okay. We'll pray for him."

The emergency medical personnel wheeled out Simon on a gurney and then loaded him onto the ambulance. Joey had tears in his eyes as he watched. As the ambulance drove off with sirens blaring, he started crying and sobbed "Grandpa, grandpa!"

Minnie took Joey to her house and told him, "You'll stay with me until your grandpa gets better and can come home."

Joey nodded, "Okay, Aunt Millie, but can we go to the hospital to see him now?"

"Of course," she said. "Let me change my clothes and we'll go over there right away."

Before they left for the hospital, Minnie phoned her sister Amelia, Simon's other sister, to let her know about what had happened. Amelia and Simon never did get along very well. In fact, they had not spoken since just after Richard and Amy had died. Amelia had called Simon a "stubborn old fool" who had no faith in God for the way he was acting. She had offended him further when, in the same verbal attack, she called him a "sinful heathen" because he quit going to church. Actually, most people avoided Amelia because of her irresponsible outspokenness. She had offended too many people, and now she was the most despised person in the neighborhood. Maybe even in the community. But Minnie, being a good person and her only sister, tolerated her and tried her best to have at least a family-level relationship.

Minnie was about to back up her car from the driveway into the street, when all of a sudden she heard a loud tapping on her window. It was Amelia. Minnie rolled down the window and Amelia said to her, "You know, I was thinking after you called me that if that old fool dies, he's gonna go to hell for turning his back on God!"

"Amelia!" Minnie said loudly. "Don't be talking like that! Joey's right here, and I don't want him hearing things like that!" Before Amelia could say anything more, Minnie quickly rolled up the window, backed up, and left.

As she drove down the street, Joey asked her, "Aunt Minnie, will grandpa really go to hell? A boy said at school that that's where people go to burn if they're bad. I don't want grandpa to burn. And he hasn't been bad, has he?"

"No, *mijo*, don't listen to your aunt Amelia," she said. "She shouldn't have said that. She's the one who's being bad."

Minnie and Joey arrived at the hospital. Joey practically jumped out of the car before it had stopped. His anxiety showed. He and Minnie walked up the stairs, but Joey almost seemed like he wanted to run.

When they had reached the lobby, Minnie immediately went to the counter where a sign read "Information." She asked the receptionist at the counter, "We want to see my brother. He was brought here by ambulance just about an hour ago." She gave the receptionist Simon's name, and waited.

The receptionist looked up Simon's information and reported back to her, "Your brother is on the critical patients list. It's written here that he cannot have any visitors yet. If you don't want to wait here and instead go home, I can take your phone number down and call you if there are any changes."

Of course, Minnie didn't want to do that, so she told the receptionist that she and Joey would wait around there. The receptionist told her that that was alright, and then told her where the bathroom was located.

Minnie and Joey sat down in the waiting room. They were motionless and quiet for a few minutes. Then Joey spoke, "Aunt Minnie?"

"Yes, *mijo*?" Joey stuttered at first, but then got the words out, "Aunt Minnie, if grandpa is mad at God, is God mad at him. too?"

"I don't think so, *mijo*. God is very understanding and patient."

Minnie thought for a few minutes. She really didn't want to talk to Joey about it because he is so young. On the other hand, she knew he was really worried about what Amelia had said, and if she knows children, he's going to continue to ask questions. She was now in a difficult situation because, if Simon ever found out about anything that she told Joey that wasn't what he would allow him to hear, he would probably keep her away from Joey and that was the last thing that she wanted.

Someone called out from behind the reception counter. "Visitor for Simon Guerra?" Minnie and Joey both quickly stood up.

The lady behind the counter, upon seeing Joey, said to Minnie, "No, I'm sorry. The boy is too young, ma'am. No children under the age of twelve in intensive care. He's not twelve, is he?"

"No, he isn't," Millie answered.

Joey pleaded, "But he's my grandpa. I promise I will be quiet. I just want to see if he's alright."

With a grimace on her face, the attendant started to say something but Minnie stopped her by putting her finger to her lips and shaking her head. The attendant then understood that Minnie didn't want her to say how bad Simon's condition really was.

Minnie looked at Joey and told him to wait there in the waiting room and she would only be a few minutes. But Joey started to cry, "All I want is to see my grandpa. Can you tell him that I'm out here, Aunt Minnie? And tell him that they won't let me in."

"Yes, I will, *mijo*. I will be right back," she said, as she walked away to where Simon's room was.

Minnie *did* only visit with Simon very briefly. Even though the doctor, who was attending Simon, told her that Simon was in critical condition and that he may not last very long, Minnie held back her emotions in order to save Joey from any more suffering that he was already experiencing.

As Minnie led Joey out of the hospital to the car, she was quiet. But Joey could not hold back his deep concern, "Is he going to die?"

Minnie thought quickly, and then said to Joey, "*Mijo*, the doctor doesn't know anything for sure yet. How about we pray for your grandpa? I think that if we both pray, God will hear us and maybe he'll get well soon."

That night, after Minnie had led Joey in prayer and then tucked him into bed, Joey again prayed silently by himself, "Please God, I know that I have not prayed before because my grandpa didn't teach me, but now I think that we both need your help. My Aunt Minnie says that you are powerful and good and that you help people if they ask. Well, I'm asking! Please help us, and I will ask grandpa if my aunt Minnie can teach me more about you and let me go to church like my friends and my cousins do."

Joey didn't want to go to school the next morning, but Minnie told him that he had to. He walked around the corner and met up with his cousin Bobby. "Hey Joey," Bobby said, not joking around like he always did. "I heard about Uncle Simon. Everybody was praying for him at my house last night."

Joey was quiet at first, but then he spoke. "Aunt Amelia said, if he dies he will go to hell. I don't want my grandpa to go to hell. If he dies, I want him to go to Heaven. Aunt Minnie says that everything is good in Heaven, and that's where we're supposed to go to rest forever. I want my grandpa to rest if he dies. I think he's sick because he's too old and tired."

When they got to school, Bobby said to Joey, "See you later. Maybe we can eat lunch together at the cafeteria, if you want."

Joey answered quietly, "Okay, Bobby. See you later".

In the classroom, Joey sat at his desk and looked around. He noticed that the room had been decorated for Christmas. *That's right*, he thought. *It's going to be Christmas.* Simon never did any Christmas celebrations in his house, but he did always give Joey a present or two.

Mrs. Brown, the teacher, asked everyone to give her their attention. Once she had everyone's attention and their eyes were away from the decorated walls, she announced, "Well, children, in another week we're going to have Christmas vacation and I'm sure that you are all looking forward to Christmas." The children all smiled and nodded yes.

Mrs. Brown couldn't help noticing the sad look on Joey's face. She knew about Simon because Millie had called the school to let them know about Simon's critical condition. She told them that Joey may need some special attention. Mrs. Brown then quickly said, "Well, guess what? This morning, I want you to write a letter to Santa Claus telling him about what you want for Christmas and why." The children cheered and applauded, but Joey just sat quietly and seemed uninterested.

Mrs. Brown asked the children to get out their pencils and she passed out paper to write their letters. The children immediately and excitedly started to write. But Joey just sat there with pencil in hand and glanced out the window. Mrs. Brown noticed him and walked over to him. "Don't you want to write your letter, Joey?" she whispered. "Well, maybe you need time to think. Let me know if you need help. Okay?"

Joey sat there and still, no letter writing. Then, an idea came to his mind. He quickly got up, but walked quietly to Mrs. Brown's desk not knowing what she would say about his idea.

As he got to her desk, Joey whispered, "Mrs. Brown? Is it okay if I write a letter to God about what I want for Christmas?" Mrs. Brown looked at him and immediately guessed why he wanted to do that. She, being a Catholic, welcomed it and was understanding of Joey's idea and immediately answered him. "Why, yes, Joey. You can do that. I think that is an excellent idea." Joey smiled, thanked her, and quickly walked back to his desk to write. Mrs. Brown, in the meantime, looked at Joey as he took his desk again and began to write. She admired him for his unselfishness and big heart. It was evident to her that Joey was very smart for his age and she saw a maturity growing in him that she had never seen before in a child who was so young.

As Joey walked home from school, he was feeling better about his grandfather's situation. He didn't know why or what it was that he was feeling, but he felt warm all over even though it was a cold day. He thought about what he had written in his letter and he felt even warmer.

Mrs. Brown was going through the letters and was enjoying reading them. Then she got to Joey's letter. She began to read it. It started with "Dear God" and tears began to form in her eyes as she read on. "An eight-year-old?" She said quietly to herself as she read. She continued to cry softly as she read. She read on and read what Joey had written: that his grandpa was a good man who had lost his loved ones, and as a result, got very weak and lost his faith in God. She read that Joey felt the losses too, even though he didn't get to know his parents or grandma, but his grandpa was his life now and he loved him more than anything or anyone in the world. He went on to say that he loved him so much that when Aunt Amelia had said what she said about his grandpa, he almost told her that *she* was the one who was going to go to hell. But out of respect for his Aunt Minnie, he held his words and felt the anger all to himself. Mrs. Brown went on to read that he was asking God to forgive his grandpa and wrote that he was sure that he didn't mean to be mad at Him and to please forgive him for he was hurting so much that he didn't realize what he was doing. He went on to say that he didn't want his grandpa to go to hell, and if God didn't send him there, he would be a good boy and a good man for the rest of his life.

Minnie received a call from the hospital. She was informed that Simon's condition had worsened and that he had gone into a coma. Immediately after the call, she called Father John and told him about Simon's condition. She asked him to go to the hospital and give the Sacrament of the "Anointing of the Sick" to Simon and that she would be there as soon as she could. Father John told her that he would leave for the hospital right way.

Minnie told Joey that they needed to go to the hospital. As she drove, Minnie thought about it quickly and then informed Joey that his grandpa's condition had worsened. Joey just said, "Okay, Aunt Minnie." Minnie was surprised that Joey seemed to be taking the news so well. She now thought that Joey was probably accepting what was probably going to happen and she felt that was good.

They arrived at the hospital and entered the lobby. Father John was in the lobby waiting for them. He looked first at Joey and then at Minnie. He quietly informed them, "Simon is with God now." Then he looked at them again, smiled, and said, "But he awoke from the coma and looked up and he said as loud as he could, 'I do believe in you and I do love you, God. Please forgive me.'"

After Simon's death, Joey went to live with his Aunt Minnie permanently and she became his legal guardian. She taught him to be a good Catholic Christian. She was very proud of him when he received his First Holy Communion, and then again when he became an altar boy. Later, they celebrated his Confirmation.

When Joey became a senior in high school, he went with his Aunt Minnie to see Father John who was now a Monsignor at St. Lucy's Catholic Church. Joey informed him that he wanted to become a priest. Monsignor helped and advised him on what he needed to do. Later, Joey succeeded and eventually became a Catholic priest. His Aunt Minnie attended his ordination ceremony and beamed with pride and joy.

Several years later, Father Joseph, as he was known now, returned to the community and became pastor at St. Lucy's Catholic Church. Six months after he had arrived, his Aunt Minnie died in her sleep at the age of eighty-five. Father Joseph, of course, celebrated her Mass and gave an unforgettable eulogy.

Father Joseph's Aunt Amelia had died five years before Minnie. He had long forgiven her. He had realized and had eventually learned that sometimes good comes out of bad things that people do or say. He felt that if it hadn't been for Aunt Amelia's irresponsible words, he may not have experienced the joy of knowing God and receiving His blessings.

As long as he lived, Father Joseph had always believed that God had indeed read his letter and had given him His blessings and to his grandpa, and then gave him a beautiful life in servitude to Him. Father Joseph had also made good his promise. The community at St. Lucy's loved him and they always talked about what a good and dedicated priest he was.

THE END

THE FEUD

Rodrigo Santos heard the bullet zing by and just missed his shoulder. He hit the ground behind an assemblage of empty wine barrels. He shouted out, "Zeke! Zeke Garcia, if that's you I'm going to kill you for sure when I find you!"

He couldn't see who it was, but knew it had to be Zeke. Who else would take a shot at him?

Rodrigo quickly reached down to his waistband where he had tucked a small .22 caliber pistol under his belt. He quickly drew it and waited.

It was quiet. Zeke had indeed gone. He was running through the vineyard with his body crouching as he ran. He knew that Rodrigo wasn't a "good shot," but when it came to guns, anything can happen.

Before he stood up, Rodrigo took a shot in the direction where the shot had come from. It hit a heavy oak barrel with an echoed "thud." His nostrils caught the smell of gunpowder.

He stood up, looked around, and aimed his pistol at a barrel. He called out again, "That you, Zeke, you snake? Show yourself, you coward!"

There was no answer. Rodrigo assumed that Zeke *was* gone. "Maybe he went back to his rathole," Rodrigo muttered. Was *he* scared? Of course, anyone who had just been shot at would be.

Rodrigo and Zeke had had it in for each other for almost a year now. Neither had even grazed the other for as many times as they had taken shots at each other. People would say that they really didn't want to kill, just scare each other. Or at least, that's the way it seemed.

Were they in disagreement over a woman? Had one cheated the other in one of the poker games that took place every Friday night at Lugo's Place?

Lugo's Place was a bar on the outskirts of town. Rodrigo and Zeke were regulars there. Men gathered there to drink, play pool, and listen to a heavyset "painted lady" sing and dance to Mexican songs that told of love, broken hearts, drinking, and hard times.

Was this a fight that was started but never finished? Or could it be that they were just two young Mexican "roosters" who couldn't stand each other?

Well, it was now 1955 and the days of the old "wild west" were pretty much gone, but these two men were acting like they were still living in those days. One takes a shot or two this week, and the other takes a shot or two the next. Always, it was just missing by a few inches. But there was one thing for sure, Rodrigo didn't miss when he shot and killed Zeke's dog Boney. The dog had attacked and killed his best fighting cock. Rodrigo had never been so angry.

After the incident happened, nothing had been the same between the two former "buddies." Before that unfortunate day, they were inseparable. They had known each other since kindergarten in this small town of Laton, California. Everyone in town thought that they were brothers, or at least cousins.

The amazing fact that they looked alike added to this unique relationship. They were both slim, of the same height, and both had straight black hair, dark brown eyes, light skin, and almost identical voices. Neither one had finished high school and neither one had married. Neither had fathered any children either, *surprisingly*. Now at age twenty-eight, they had both grown big heavy moustaches and had let their hair grow to shoulder length. Also, they both liked wearing blue jeans and checkered long-sleeved flannel shirts. They both wore a large black feather in their hatbands. But if it wasn't for the red bandanas that Rodrigo liked to wear around his neck and the dark glasses that Zeke sometimes wore, they could almost pass for twins, or for sure, look-a-likes.

As they grew up into being men, they frequented bars together and had even fought side by side when either one found trouble. Once, as the story goes, Rodrigo went to jail for something that Zeke had done. Taking the "rap" for Zeke was how Rodrigo proved his loyalty and dedication to their friendship. Zeke had never forgotten that. Until that day Rodrigo shot his beloved dog.

On the other hand, Rodrigo became understandably enraged at the "murder" of his prize rooster, his pride and joy. On top of that, it was a good source of income for Rodrigo. It all proved to be devastating to this once unique "brotherhood."

At his dog's burial, Zeke vowed, with tears streaming down his face, that he would get even with Rodrigo even if it meant killing his "ex-friend." Rodrigo, on the other hand, claimed that justice had been served and that the Holy Bible was the law, as far as he was concerned. "An eye for an eye and a tooth for a tooth!" That was what Rodrigo had screamed in answer after Zeke found his dog and had demanded for Rodrigo to tell who shot him.

Although today didn't seem any different than any other, there was an uncertain mystical cloud of anxiety that hung in the air. It even had a chill to it. It was only fall and there was no reason for it to be that cold yet. But then again, it was one of those days that any person who had any sense of psychic ability would unfortunately say that it was a bad day for the sun to rise. Not everyone felt it, but those who did like Mary Soto, who owned the ranch and winery where Rodrigo and Zeke worked, had an uneasy feeling that something was going to happen that day. And it didn't feel like it was going to be something good.

Rodrigo shrugged, shook his head, and walked toward the vineyard. It was almost quitting time. He was going to finish hoeing down some weed under some vines and then go home.

A large crow landed on a vine and cawed loudly, as if taunting Rodrigo. He picked up a dirt clod and flung it at the big black bird. It flew off cawing in the distance.

As he bent down to pick up the hoe that he had been working with, a shadow appeared. He suddenly heard Zeke's grim voice, "Now I've got you, punk!" He was standing there with his gun aimed at Rodrigo. Rodrigo quickly reached for his gun and aimed it at Zeke. Zeke was astonished, but neither said a word as they stood there facing each other.

What happened next and exactly how it happened, no one knows or will ever know. They were completely alone. No one was around to hear what they had to say to each other or what they didn't have to say. The perfect moment and the perfect place had arrived.

Bam! Bam! Both guns went off at the same time. There was the smell of gunpowder with light white smoke in the air.

The two had shot each other near the middle of their chests. They staggered and then fell to the ground. Nothing could be more cynical to such a relationship. Early in their lives, they had walked, run, and laughed together as children. Now, they were falling to the ground as feuding men—with bullets in their hearts.

After a few quiet minutes as they lay bleeding and obviously dying, Zeke spoke up, coughing and struggling, "R-Rodrigo?"

"Yeah, man?"

"You 'member that time you took that rap for me?"

"Yeah, a-ah 'member."

"Well t'anks, man."

"D-don't menshen it, man."

It was quiet now. The two lay motionless. Suddenly, their souls emerged from their bodies *at the same time*. They stood suspended in midair. They looked down at their bodies lying in the vineyard. They glanced at each other. They smiled and then they nodded. It was over.

Rodrigo's soul started ascending. He said to Zeke, "You comin', bud?"

Zeke took a deep breath and sighed, "Yeah, man. Let's go, bud."

As they continued to ascend, Rodrigo said, "Do you think God will punish us for this and not let us into heaven?"

"Nah," said Zeke. "God is forgiving. He'll probably chew us out, though."

It was late afternoon. The sun started to set in a brilliant reddish burst of rays.

The crow returned. It landed on a vine and looked at the bodies. It cawed at them loudly, and then flew off cawing and ascending to join a flock of crows flying overhead. The flock joined in the cawing, and then noisily circled a large tree where they were to roost for the night.

For the rest of the night, the murder of crows was quiet. There were two that perched together and apart from the rest. They closed their eyelids over their bloodshot eyes, and without a sound, fell asleep.

For days, the community talked about Zeke and Rodrigo. Some would say that they went straight to hell for what they did. Others, on the other hand, would say what Zeke had said: that God is forgiving. And since the two men did believe in God, it was very probable that they were forgiven, although they would probably not enter Heaven right away. Only God knows. That's for sure.

THE END

THE RIVER

Looking at it from a bird's-eye view, the Kings River that runs through Kings and Fresno Counties in the great San Joaquin Valley, as well as other counties, looks like a great shiny snake, as the sun gleams its light on it as it meanders through the countryside. Lined with borders of trees and plants of different varieties on the banks, it appears to be protected from the heat of the Valley in hot summer days. It's a river that has its own deep and interesting history. It gives off a mystical feeling that even today gives me a strange feeling of wonderment. I sometimes wonder and imagine what might be out there and what it might be like to walk around out there at night when it should be quiet, still, and lifeless.

Brothers Johnny and Joey and their cousins Rachel and Ronnie were bored. It was summer and school had just let out a week ago for the summer vacation. They didn't feel that there was much to do in Laton these days.

They had outgrown "hide and seek" and "tag, you're it." Hanging around the playground playing baseball or basketball was limited to the morning hours because of the heat in the afternoon which could reach as high as 105 degrees.

Johnny was thirteen years old now going on fourteen, Joey was eleven, and twins Rachel and Ronnie were also eleven years old.

Johnny was going to attend Laton High School in the fall. Joey, Rachel, and Ronnie were going to attend Laton-Conejo Elementary School again. They had decided to make the most of *this* summer vacation because, when school starts with various new school activities, they were not going to see each other as often as they had. They had always been close cousins like brothers and a sister. Their fathers were brothers and their mothers were sisters, and so they were close families that even took vacations together. Their families had homes just down the street from each other on De Woody Street. But, it was going to be at least three weeks before they were going on a planned vacation to Kaweah Lake in Tulare County. Last summer, the families had gone to Pismo Beach on the central coast of California, and that had been a great time for everyone. This year since the kids were older, their parents had decided to take them camping and go boating, fishing, and swimming in the lake.

Rachel spoke up, "Hey, guys, it's almost noon. Why don't we go get some stuff at the store and go to the river? We can go swimming 'cause it's starting to get hot. Maybe if we go early we can get a good spot under the shade."

It was a Friday, and usually on Fridays, some people get off early from work and take their families to the river for a picnic and for swimming. Somebody had strung up a rope with an old rubber tire on a tree on the south bank of the river. The river was deeper there, so people would swing onto the river from the tire and then swim back out to wait for their turn again.

Johnny, Joey, and the twins were warned by their parents about going to the river without them, even though they knew that they were all good swimmers. They had all belonged to a swim club in nearby Hanford and participated in several swim meets around Kings County. Johnny had won several first place ribbons, and so was sometimes referred to by his proud father as "champ."

It was known that the river had taken many lives by drownings over the past several years. It was especially dangerous for children, since most are not good, strong swimmers and it did not take much time for a child to wander into deep and fast moving water and get carried away when a parent's attention was diverted elsewhere. The river was especially dangerous when in the first early months of hot weather when the snow packs in the Sierra-Nevada Mountains would begin to melt quickly. The water is then released from the dam near the Three Rivers Area, thereby causing the river to run frighteningly fast and rise to high and dangerous levels everywhere. The cold water and the dangerous almost invisible undercurrents made it difficult to swim in. The water could carry away any person, even a good swimmer.

Johnny, Joey, and the twins went into their homes to change into swimwear and to get towels. Their dog Raggs, a mixed terrier, followed Johnny and Joey into their house. Joey said to Johnny, "Hey, let's take Raggs, too! He'll like getting in the water, too. Won't you, Raggs?" Raggs looked at Joey, and with his tongue hanging out and his tail wagging, let out a soft whine.

Johnny and Joey met the twins out in the street. The twins lived just across the street from the store, so they just met in front of the twins' house and then walked across the street to the store. They walked inside and started to shop for their "stuff" that they would share for lunch. Johnny picked up a large bag of potato chips. Joey picked up a bag of marshmallows, and Ronnie reached into the walk-in box and got four plastic bottles of punch. Rachel picked up two bags of beef jerky. The shopping was done. They paid for their food and walked out of the store and back out into the street, with Raggs following and wagging his tail. He knew that they had food, and he knew that he was going to eat some of it, too.

As the children walked along the street, the day was starting to get hotter. They could feel the heat from the asphalt pavement and so they walked along the dirt shoulder. As they got to Latonia Street, they saw Jenny, a friend and classmate of Rachel's, sitting on the porch of her home.

"Hi, Jenny," they all said.

"Hi," she responded.

Rachel told her, "We're going to the river. Wanna come along?"

"No, I can't," said Jenny. "I'm waiting for mom to come home from work to take me to the dentist in Hanford."

"Oh," said Rachel. "I hope you're not getting any drilling." "No," said Jenny. "Just teeth cleaning."

"Okay," said Rachel.

"We'll see you later then. Say hi to Ricky."

"Okay," said Jenny.

They all waved goodbye to each other and started on their trip to the River again. But before long, Ronnie started teasing his sister with a high-pitched voice, "Ricky, Ricky." The kids all knew that Jenny's brother Ricky had a crush on Rachel. "Oh," said Rachel. "You're just jealous 'cause Ricky's cute." With that, the boys all started to laugh and teased her about Ricky. Johnny made his voice high-pitched and teased Rachel, "Ricky, Ricky, you're *so* cute!" The other two boys laughed. Rachel, red-faced but not from the sun's heat, just walked and covered her ears.

As they were getting to the river, the kids noticed that there were already several cars parked along the road that crosses the river. This meant that there were already many people at the river. As they got closer, they saw that indeed there *were* many people there. The air was filled with the noise of kids laughing and shrieking as they played and splashed in the water. Raggs barked, and Johnny said to him, "Okay, boy, you'll be getting in there real soon."

As the kids found a spot, they laid out their towels to sit on and rest from their walk in the heat. Their parents had told them before that they should not get into the water right away if they had been in the heat, and that they should cool off first by just sitting on the beach or by the bank of the river for a few minutes. But of course they didn't tell Raggs anything, so he went scampering in the low water. Then he went swimming and came out wet and was shaking off the water near the kids. They all shouted at him "Hey, that water's cold!" as he shook some of that cold river water on them.

After a few minutes, when they have rested and cooled off a bit, the boys challenged each other to a race and went running into the water. "Aah!" shouted Johnny. "It feels good! Come on in, Rachel," he shouted to Rachel, who was still sitting on her towel. "Okay," she said. "But nobody better try to dip me under or I'll slap you!" The boys all laughed. They weren't going to do that because they knew, as their fathers had told them, that they had to watch over her because she was a girl. They wouldn't hesitate to tease her, but to rough her up was not something they would ever do because she was too nice to be mean to. For her age, Rachel was good at baking, and these three boys were her fans especially when it came to her peanut butter cookies which was their favorite and what she baked often.

It was now getting to be late in the afternoon. As the kids lay on their towels resting after swimming and before starting back to their homes, they started to talk.

Joey said, "I wonder what it looks like out here at night. I'll bet it's real quiet and you can probably see some of the animals that live out here like raccoons and skunks."

"Yeah, and maybe alligators, too," laughed Ronnie.

"Or maybe a 'creature of the lagoon' like I saw on a movie," joked Johnny.

"Oh," said Rachel. "There are no such things as 'creatures of the lagoon' and there aren't any alligators out here either."

"Well," said Johnny. "Maybe we ought to come out here some night and see what *is* out here."

"Yeah! How about tonight?" said Joey. "The moonlight should be good since there will be a half moon tonight."

"Yeah, well, you'll have to sneak out because our parents sure won't let you come out here at night," said Rachel.

"Well, okay, let's do that then," said Ronnie. "We'll wait until our parents are asleep and we'll sneak out the window."

"Well," said Rachel. "I'm coming, too, if you're coming Ronnie."

"No, I don't think so," said Johnny. "Our parents will really get mad then if we brought you along because you're a girl."

"Hey!" said Rachel. "I'm just as adventuresome as you guys, and this could be an adventure. I'll tell you what, if you'll let me come too, I'll bake a peach pie for you guys and I'll get some vanilla ice cream to go with it."

The boys all looked at each other. They didn't hesitate and they all said in unison, "Okay."

That night, the kids all went to bed a little early. Johnny said that he would wake up late in the night, wake up Joey, and then sneak out to the twins' house where they were to meet. They had talked earlier and decided that they would take a couple of flashlights, some sticks in case they ran into any wild animals like alligators, and Raggs for added protection.

That night about 10:30 p.m. after their parents finally went to sleep, Johnny got up and was going to wake Joey up, but he was already awake. "I couldn't sleep," said Joey. "Just for a little while, then I couldn't sleep anymore." "Yeah me, too," said Johnny. They got dressed and went quietly out through the window, with Johnny carrying Raggs. Once outside, they saw Rachel and Ronnie standing outside their house.

They walked over to them, and Johnny whispered, "How long have you been out here?"

"We just came out," whispered Rachel. "Our parents fell asleep early in front of the TV and then went to bed."

As they walked through the street, Johnny said to them, "Hey listen you guys, keep a look out for the deputy that patrols Laton. If anybody sees him, let us know quietly and we'll all duck behind something."

"Okay," they all responded.

Night in the San Joaquin Valley in the summer is not always cool, and this night was no exception. It was warm. A light breeze came and went as if the night had a breath. The sky was clear, with a light blanket of stars and there *was* a bright half-moon as Joey had said there would be. Joey loved to study science. It was his favorite subject, and he was considered to be an advanced student by his teachers.

As the kids walked through the streets of Laton, they noticed that there were lights on in some of the houses. Some dogs barked as they walked by because of Raggs. They could smell him. Raggs, however, did not make a sound. Johnny called him "good boy" and dropped down some leftover chips to him. They didn't see any cars until they got close to the river. It was probably just someone going home from a late job in Hanford or Lemoore.

As they got to the bridge, they could hear the flow of the water and smell the plants with yellow flowers on them that lined the river, which they had seen many times. They walked down the embankment and they started walking on the sand. They noticed that the water level had dropped. This meant that somewhere along the line, the river had been slowed considerably, probably for irrigation uses.

As the kids walked along the river, Johnny suggested that they stop and take a break on the sandy beach. Raggs whined a little as he looked toward some bushes on the bank of the river as if he had seen someone. Joey, thinking it might just be some raccoon or possum, joked, "If anybody sees the 'creature from the lagoon,' let us know so we can run like the devil was after us." Everyone laughed. Then, they heard a giggle. Raggs growled.

"What was that?" asked Rachel.

"I think somebody's over there," said Johnny. It was not unusual that young people went to the river at night to drink beer or just fool around, but the giggle sounded like a child's. Johnny asked, looking at the bushes, "Who's there?" A figure that appeared to be that of a child's ran from along and behind the bushes. The kids all got up and went to look. Suddenly, a girl about Rachel's age but a bit smaller in height appeared.

"Hey! What are you doing here?" asked Johnny.

"I'm looking for my mother," she answered in a soft voice.

"Your mother?" asked Rachel. "Is she out here?"

"Yes, but I can't find her," the girl answered.

"We're all looking for our mothers," she said.

"Who else is looking for their mother?" Joey asked.

"Them, too," the girl answered, pointing to the bushes.

Just then, three more children came out from the bushes: two young boys and a small girl. None of the children appeared to be brothers or sisters, and they appeared to be of different ages with the little girl appearing to be about two or three years old. They were all dressed in bathing suits and had uncombed and dangling hair like they had been swimming.

Johnny, Joey, Ronnie, and Rachel were speechless. Then, Rachel spoke up, "You mean that you are all lost from your mothers?"

"No," the oldest girl said. "*They* are lost because we can't find them."

"Well then, how long have you been looking for them? Were they together?" asked Rachel, now getting very concerned.

"No," the girl said. "We have been looking for them for a very long time and they were not together," the girl answered.

Johnny then said, "Well, maybe you should come with us and we can get the Sheriff's Deputy to help you find them."

"No," the girl responded. "If we leave, our mothers might come and get worried if we are not here."

Johnny, Joey, and the twins then looked at each other. Johnny was about to say something when he looked to where the group of kids were standing and noticed that they were not there anymore. Johnny said, "Hey, they're gone!"

The others looked around, and Rachel then said, "Hey! We need to find them."

They spread out and looked everywhere and tried calling out to them but without going too far. They could not locate any of the kids. They seemed to have just vanished in the cool air of the river.

Johnny said to the rest of the group, "I don't know what this is, but it almost seems as if we just imagined them being here."

Rachel said, "Yeah, I wonder where they went so fast. I wonder if someone's playing a trick on us."

"If that's so, it's a mean trick because we were just trying to help some kids find their mothers. Why would anybody play a trick on us like that?" asked Joey.

As they were leaving the river, Johnny noticed that Raggs wasn't with them. "Raggs!, Raggs!" he called out. Suddenly, Raggs barked and came out of the bushes. "Where were you, boy?" Johnny asked the dog. Raggs just looked back at the bushes, whined softly, and then went with the kids.

Walking back to their homes, the kids were quiet and each trying to figure out what had happened. Then Johnny said, "Listen, guys, we can't tell our parents about this. But tomorrow, we should go see Zeke and ask him what we should do about those kids. If this is for real and they *are* lost, we really need to help them. They can't be alone out there like that."

Zeke was their friend and had been an old school teacher in Riverdale, another small town west of Laton. He had always been good to the kids and had helped them many times when they needed him. He had even taught them to play chess, and he sometimes personally coached the boys in sports such as baseball and basketball. Zeke was retired now and lived in the outskirts of town in an old house on Fowler Avenue, going out of Laton to Fresno. He had a large garden, two dogs, some geese, and a few chickens. He continually worked on this house just to have something to do.

On Saturday morning which was the day after the kids had been at the river and had encountered "the kids of the River" as they now called them, Johnny woke up Joey and told him that they should have some breakfast, call the twins, and have them meet them for a trip to Zeke's.

After calling the twins and a quick breakfast, Johnny and Joey dashed out of the house with Raggs following, and met up with the twins. "Well, let's go," said Johnny to the other kids. Off they went. It was as if they were going off to visit the "Wizard of Oz."

As the kids arrived at Zeke's, Zeke's dogs barked until they recognized who they were and then started wagging their tails. The dogs sniffed Raggs and then after realizing that they knew him too, just wagged their tails and trotted around the yard with him.

Hearing the dogs barking, Zeke came out of the house. When he saw who they were, he called out, "Hi, kids! I heard the dogs and wondered who had come by. What brings you out here so early?"

"Well," said Johnny. "We were at the river last night and we saw something kind of weird."

"Out at the river at night? Did your parents know that you were out there at night?" asked Zeke.

"Yeah, I know," responded Johnny. "We shouldn't have been out there. And no, our parents did not know. Please, don't tell them. But let me tell you what happened."

"Let's go inside," said Zeke. The kids went inside with Zeke, sat with him in the living room of his home, and told him what had happened.

"Well," said Zeke, sighing and scratching his chin. "Sounds strange, alright. And you say you *all* saw those kids? I can only say that they had to be real kids which is a real serious concern, or they were ghosts which may be another serious concern."

"Ghosts?" gasped the kids as they looked at each other.

"Well now," said Zeke. "It can only be one of two answers that I can think of. But you know what? Maybe you ought to go see Maria."

"You mean that old woman who lives in that spooky old house on the other side of town with all the junk in the front yard? People say she's a witch," said Johnny.

"Well, she's not a witch," said Zeke. "She's a religious woman and people misunderstand her, but she's actually very wise."

"Oh!" said Joey. "Can she tell the future and can she communicate with spirits and stuff like that?"

"No, not that. She prays for people and knows the Bible pretty well, but I think that she's the person that can help you," said Zeke. "Why don't you go over and see her? And don't be afraid. I know that she won't hurt you. People have the wrong idea about her because they really don't know her. But I'll call her and tell her that I sent you over."

As they left, Johnny said, "Well, if Zeke said that it'll be okay, then I guess it's okay to go over there." They made their way across town until they reached Maria's house. There was a gate at the front fence of the property, but it wasn't locked. Then Johnny started to enter when Rachel said, "Oh, now I'm scared."

"You don't have go in if you're scared," said Johnny.

"Well, I don't want to stand out here by myself, either," said Rachel. "So I guess I'll go in, too." Johnny walked up to the door and knocked. A dog that sounded like a small dog barked furiously inside. Then a lady was heard telling the dog,

"Quiet, Jiggy. It's just some kids." She opened the door and looked at the kids. Then she asked, "Are you the kids that Zeke sent over?"

Johnny answered nervously, "Yes, ma'am, that's us."

"Well come in," said the lady. The kids stepped in, but they left Raggs outside. Maria led them to a dining room in the middle of the house. They noticed that the house was cluttered with many things, much of which were books, some boxes, some old furniture, old lamps, stacks of papers, and a pile of what looked like unused new dishes.

She asked them to sit at the large dining table which could seat eight people. "Well," she said. "Zeke told me that you saw some children out at the river last night. First, as anybody will tell you, children like you or *any* child do not belong out there without adult supervision. Especially at night."

She sounds like a grandma, Johnny thought to himself. That made him feel better about her and he didn't feel too nervous anymore.

"We know," said Johnny apologetically.

"Well, please don't ever do that again," said Maria.

The kids all said, "Okay."

"Alright. Now tell me what you saw," said Maria.

The kids told her about their experience and how they were concerned.

"Well, let me tell you," Maria began. "You are not the first who have seen these children. I have heard that others have seen them, but you are the first who care enough to find out what can be done for them. But then, it was meant to be this way. You see, some people think that they were Indian children ghosts because there were Yokut Indians who inhabited the area a long time ago. Some lived by the river. I think no one wanted to say very much about it or do anything because they thought that that area was sacred burial ground or something. But that is not what this is. They are children who drowned in the river over the past several years. They are ghosts because they all drowned in the river and died tragically or traumatically, which means that they all suffered shock. The oldest girl drowned because she ran away from home for the day and then went swimming, but she was not a good swimmer. She drowned being sorry that she got angry with her mother. The three-year-old child was intentionally drowned by her mother's jealous boyfriend many, many years ago. He claimed that he tried to save her, but he lied. Yes, she was murdered. The two boys that you saw drowned when the river level was high and running fast. They were on rubber tubes and an undercurrent caught them from under and caused them to overturn. They had gone there without permission from their parents. No, no one was being punished by God. God is loving and forgiving. The river is not a bad place to be, but it should be respected. It is dangerous for anybody when they are not careful around any water, be it a river, a canal, a ditch, a lake, or the ocean. That's why we adults keep telling our kids to be careful. And most of all, to listen to us and obey us because we really do know better."

Johnny, Joey, and the twins sat silently. They seemed to be shocked, sad, and then remorseful for going out there at night. And now, even going out there during the day by themselves. They seemed to be facing a reality that many kids don't know because they don't have the exposure to see and understand for themselves the perils that await children in a world and life that can be dangerous.

"Well," Johnny spoke up quietly. "Can anything be done about those kids?"

"I am glad that you are concerned," said Maria. "Because you have already started to help by caring and wanting to help. And Zeke will help, too. You see, Zeke also lost a child in the river. He also lost his beautiful wife. The child went too far in the water and was carried away. Her mother frantically jumped in to save her but she was carried away, too. They both drowned. Zeke was teaching in Laton at the time. But after that happened, he went to teach in Riverdale because his wife was also a teacher in Laton. She had the classroom next to his, and their child was a student in her class. There were too many memories there."

Maria said to the kids, "Now, I am ready to give you kids instructions on what you must do. Yes, I said 'what you must do' because you're the only ones who can help them."

"Why only us?" asked Rachael.

"Because you are children like them. Children understand other children better. You see, I know that because I was a teacher, too. The goodness that you each possess is important, too, because this effort and concern on your part comes from your caring, loving hearts and young but good souls. You need to go out there again and tell the children that they must go to the light and go over to the other side where they belong. I will get Zeke to get permission from your parents, and he will go out there with you. I know that they will understand and let you go out there. They are very good people and they will believe in what you have to do. Zeke cannot go talk to the children. They will only come out to you and only listen to you because they will only listen to you children. I will help by praying for the children and you."

Maria had called Zeke, and Zeke visited the kids' parents that afternoon to explain to them about what had happened. He then asked them for permission for the kids to go out to the river that night and do what had to be done. Although the parents were very concerned, they were cooperative and said that they would go to church to pray for their children and for "the river kids." The mothers were especially sorrowful for "the river kids'" plight. They knew what it is to be mothers, and that nothing could more heartbreaking than losing a child to death.

Late that night, Zeke picked up Johnny, Joey, and the twins in his car. After saying good-bye to their parents, the kids got in the car with Zeke and sat silently all the way to the river. When they arrived, Zeke told them, "Okay. You know that I can't go with you, so I'll wait up here on the bank by the bridge. Take this flashlight. You may not need it since the moonlight is good tonight. Be careful, stick together, and don't go too far. Raggs can go with you. I don't think he will be any problem. In fact, he will probably sense the kids if they are out there."

As always, Johnny led the group down the bank and onto the river's beach. As they walked silently, an owl hooted in one of the trees. The moonlight was indeed bright and it gave the river a glistening look as it flowed. The odor of the willows was strong now. Something moved around in the bushes and the group stopped, but then they saw a cat dash out and then it ran away to another clump of bushes. Raggs whined but did not bark. It was as if he knew that he shouldn't make any noise.

They walked a distance and then Johnny decided that they had gone as far as they should. "Let's stop here," he said. "Maybe we ought to just sit here and wait to see if they come out." They sat on the sand silently and looked around for about a half hour.

Then Joey whispered, "What if they don't come out?"

Johnny answered, "Yeah, well, we can't be out here all night. Maybe we ought to call for them." Then he called out without shouting, "Kids, are you here? If you are, come out. It's us again."

After a few minutes, Johnny said, "Maybe they aren't going to come out. Maybe they went somewhere else. Let's go, guys." He got up and the other kids got up, too. Suddenly, Raggs whined softly while looking toward some bushes.

Johnny looked at the bushes, and then said, "Hey, are you there, kids?"

Suddenly, the girl came out with the other three kids behind her. "Have you seen our mothers?" she asked softly.

"No," answered Johnny. but you must go to the light and to the 'other side.' Your mothers might be there waiting for you." The girl looked at Johnny then at Rachel.

Rachel then spoke to her, "He's right. You must go to the light and go to the 'other side.' That's where you belong."

The girl said, "Okay." She then turned around, led the group back into the bushes, and they disappeared. Rachel and Ronnie started to cry softly. Johnny then put one arm around each of their shoulders and said, "Come on, guys. I think they'll be okay now."

They walked back to where Zeke was pacing nervously near the bridge. "Is everyone okay? Did you see them?" asked Zeke when they got closer.

"Yes sir," said Johnny, with his arms still around the twins. "We're okay and I think we did it," said Johnny. "I can feel that we did, and I feel good about it."

"Good," said Zeke. "Now let's get you all home to your parents. They're probably very worried."

As they rode back to their homes with Zeke, the kids had smiles on their faces. They expressed to Zeke that they didn't really feel afraid out there. They were more worried that "the river kids" weren't going to show up. They felt that they had indeed done a good thing for some other children and they felt proud that it was them that were apparently "chosen" by God to do this important job. They had been told by a teacher who taught Sunday school at their church that sometimes "God works in mysterious ways." Ghosts were not much of a mystery to them now. They had realized now that they must be souls who could not find their way to "the other side." They were happy and felt good that they were able to help "the river kids."

Sometimes we feel fear in our experiences. We fear what we don't know. We find consolation and a sense of gratitude in our hearts when we are able to help other souls in need, because that's who we really are: souls in need, souls in need of each other, and souls who need to find and make our way back home where we belong.

Four years later, after Johnny had graduated from Laton High School and had just turned eighteen, he was driving to his night job in Hanford. As he started to pass over the bridge at the river, he heard a noise under the hood of his parents' car. He pulled over on the shoulder past the bridge overlooking the river. He got out with a flashlight and was going to open the hood when he realized that the hood was open and not latched. He realized that it was the noise of the loose and vibrating hood that he had heard. He pushed down on the hood until it was latched. He started to get back into the car when something caught his eyes. On the south bank of the river in the moonlight, he saw two children in swimsuits looking at him. Then they disappeared into the bushes. Johnny said to himself with a sigh, *Here we go again*. And drove off to work.

THE END

THE TRACKS: SHOOTING STARS

Ever since I was a kid, whenever I hear a train horn blowing in the night especially when I lay awake in bed, I wonder where that train was going and who's on it and where are they going. It's freight trains that I really think about. They seem to be the ones with "personality." Sometimes, depending how close I am, other than the roar and rumble of the engine, I can hear the "clack-clack- clack-clack" of the steel wheels as they pass over the cracks where the lengths of railroad tracks meet. It's as if the train is on a determined journey and a mission to crack through the dark of the night to greet daylight for another bright day of life.

It's going to be a "scorcher" today, thought Sonny, as he walked along the side of the Santa Fe railroad tracks. Being July in Hanford in the San Joaquin Valley of Central California, it wasn't unusual that the afternoon temperature might reach 103 to 110 degrees. But to Sonny, it always seemed hotter when walking along the tracks. Maybe it was because of the rock bed where the heavy steel tracks lay. Today, he was only wearing a white T-shirt, jeans, and a Panama hat because he had expected the intense summer heat.

Walking was Sonny's only way to get around whenever he wasn't "hopping freights." He thought nothing of it since he had been doing this since he "left in 1940." *This is the life of a "hobo,"* he thought, as he trudged along the base of the slope from the tracks in jaunting steps, carrying his few belongings. Not really going anywhere that he needed to be today, Sonny wasn't in a hurry . . . just going.

Sonny came from Oklahoma and that's all anyone needed to know. As far as he was concerned, he didn't even want to remember where he came from or why he was here now. He left Oklahoma in 1940 and now it was July 11, 1945, although he didn't really know that. Remembering was one thing that Sonny didn't want to do. And as far as he was concerned, "just moving on" was the only thing that he cared about now.

Today, as he just arrived from Fresno, Sonny wasn't going to the "hobo jungle" in southwest Hanford next to the Southern Pacific railroad tracks.

He thought he would just head for his favorite camping spot in Hanford, and that was along the tracks that backed up to Don Diego's property which fronted Phillips Street. It was there that he could find some peace aside from an occasional passing train, and then hopefully, he might see Don Diego. He would have a chat with him over the four-foot barbed wire fence that separated Don Diego's property and the railway as he did several times over the past five years or so.

Don Diego, a short man who appeared to be in his forties, was of Mexican descent, soft-spoken, and spoke English with a heavy accent. Although quiet, Sonny found him to be the kindest person he ever met in his travels and maybe the kindest human being, without any doubt. He could tell that Don Diego was an intelligent man and a "respecting man." He never asked Sonny where he was from or even what his last name was or anything personal about him. They just talked—about anything and everything that was interesting at that moment.

As he headed south along the tracks, Sonny decided that he would go into one of the small grocery stores along Third Street or Fourth Street to get a few things that he would need to make meals later on. He felt into his pants pocket to check for some loose change. He kept his bills in a small pouch in his large burlap bag where he carried his most important belongings. Although not well off by any means, he had enough money to last him a few days. With this, he would buy canned food like beans, soup, canned sardines, and juices. He would also buy saltine crackers, salt, a loaf of French bread, matches, and if available, his favorite treat, a piece of fruit or two. Sonny didn't care much for coffee and it wasn't always available anyway, so it wasn't anything he really cared about.

Some things were hard to get these days because of the war. During this so-called World War II, many things were scarce. The government rationed many needed items including food, which many Americans once took for granted. Gasoline, meat, coffee, salt, butter, and even sugar were some of the items that a person needed "ration cards" for in order to purchase them. But a person or family could only get so many, and the government required citizens to register for the "ration cards" at designated centers.

Maybe this terrible war was going to end soon. In April, Italy's leader and dictator Benito Mussolini had been captured and hanged by Italian partisans. Germany's leader and dictator Adolf Hitler had committed suicide in April. The German forces then surrendered in May. The Allies had already taken over Germany and divided it, and official victory in Europe by the Allies had been declared. Japan, one of the other "axis powers" was next, but no one really knew what that outcome would be.

Sonny walked into a store and started looking around for what he needed. The store clerk, a portly red-faced lady who kept wiping perspiration from her face and neck, looked at Sonny and just nodded. Sonny returned the nod. He had always tried to look "decent" when he needed to go into a community. Except for his pouch with his bills, he left everything just outside the door. No one ever took his "stuff," and so he never worried about it.

Sonny was always frugal and did his best to shop for only what he needed. He had worked hard for his money at different temporary jobs. He only asked for and took handouts when it really became necessary, and even then, he was always polite and said "please" "could you please help me out" and "thank you." No "God bless you!" No "I didn't like to do that because many other hobos did that just to say it." He just accepted what he was given, said "thank you," and left. And he never kept going back to the same place because that was not the right thing to do and he might wear away the welcome and "kill" the generosity. Generally, as a "hobo," you never abuse anyone's generosity. That is what Sonny and his peers believed in and practiced.

The store had a strong scent of the oiled wood shavings and sawdust that were used on cement floors to collect dirt and debris when the floors were swept at closing time. The "gondolas," as they were called, were stocked with canned and packaged food goods. *Pinatas* hung from the ceiling. This was a neighborhood where many Mexican families lived. At the back of the store, there were cold boxes called "walk-in boxes" because a storekeeper could walk into the box to stock it with cold drinks such as sodas, beer, and milk.

Sonny gathered his goods in his hands and arms, and walked to the counter. He asked the lady if the store carried dried prunes. She answered, "Not yet. We expect that we might get some from the guy who drives in from Fresno on Fridays."

Sonny then said, "Okay, then I'll be back Friday."

Sonny paid for his goods and walked out of the store. He put his food in one of his bags, returned to the street, and walked west toward the tracks. As he walked, he looked around to see if there had been any changes since he was last in Hanford. *Nope,* he thought. *Nothing's really changed.* Sonny did not really like changes. If there was anything that changed, it would be noticeable because this is a small city. Sonny supposed that here everyone probably knew each other and that many people were probably "blood-related."

As he walked along the tracks again, he would from time to time look back. He didn't want to have a train "sneak up" on him, even though they usually made a lot of noise. On the third time that he looked back, he could see someone else walking along the tracks in the distance coming in his direction. He wondered if it was someone he knew. *Maybe, he's going to the "hobo jungle,"* he thought.

As he arrived at his destination at the spot behind Don Diego's property, he looked back again and noticed that the person was still coming. Sonny could see that he was carrying a bag and was using a walking stick. He could see that he was wearing a medium-brimmed black hat, blue baggy overalls, and a light blue shirt. He looked medium in built and appeared to be a Caucasian man older than himself. He appeared to have a slight limp, but was walking pretty steadily.

As the man came a few yards closer, Sonny greeted him by nodding up with his head and saying, "Howdy, partner!"

The man approached and responded with, "Hiyah!"

Sonny could now see that he was indeed an older man and looked like he had been through a lot in a rough life.

"My name's Sonny," Sonny said, standing and shaking the man's hand without smiling because he was not yet sure about this person.

The man responded with, "Muh name's Casey. Casey Stevens. Um from Texas and ah just got here from Fresno."

"Yeah?" said Sonny. "I just got in from Fresno, too."

"Mind if I set a spell, Sonny?" Casey asked.

"Don't mind if you do, Casey," Sonny answered, with a little more trust in his voice.

"Care to have something to eat Casey?" Sonny asked.

"No thanks," Casey answered. "Ah had leftover crackers and cheese from yesterday, and ah ate when ah was walkin'. You go ahead and eat. Don't let me get in your way. If you have any coffee, though, ah wouldn't mind some."

"I don't have any," said Sonny, not mentioning that he did not like coffee very much. Sonny actually carried coffee sometimes if he could get it because he sometimes went to the hobo jungle where he often shared what he had with other hobos. Whenever he went over there, it was a big "get together." Everyone had something to share, even if it was just crackers, cheese, and sardines. They would enjoy a hobo feast and socialize.

Sonny and Casey started to feel the earth tremble. Casey said, "Well, there's one a'comin." He meant that a train was coming their way from the north and it should be on them soon. Neither one of them had any intentions of "hopping" this train. At this point, the train would be traveling at a high speed and there was no way that anyone could get on at that speed.

The train was soon passing, making such a thundering noise that Sonny and Casey just sat and looked. Not even shouting would help if they were to try. But that was the way it was and they always respected the train and the tracks.

After the train passed, the "clack-clack-clack-clack" sounds became more and more distant and soon they faded away completely. Sonny asked Casey, "Been to Hanford before?"

"No," Casey answered. "Ah never have been here, but ah heard that they got peaches to pick out here now so ah thought ah would give 'er a try."

"Yeah, that's right. It's peach picking season," Sonny said. "But if you have never picked peaches before, you need to know that it's hard work if you can't stand the heat and the fuzz at the same time."

"Oh yeah, ah heard about that, too," Casey answered. "But ah heard that a fella could make some good money if he's willin' to work hard for a while. Ah heard too that that fuzz could give a fella a good spell of the itches and scratches."

Sonny gave Casey his experienced advise. "Yeah, I myself once got pretty bad with that fuzz. Maybe I'm allergic. Most people use powder with a bandana around the neck, if you can get the powder. But you gotta watch that you don't get it in your eyes, because if the fuzz gets around the eye lids, not only will they itch a lot but they can also swell up. So if that happens, don't rub your eyes. Makes things worse, you know."

Sonny then said to Casey, "See that vineyard there?"
"Yeah," Casey answered.
"Well, it belongs to my friend Don Diego and his family and I'm going to stick around until the end of summer to work for Don Diego during the grape harvest. Now that's a good job because, besides picking grapes, Don Diego will sometimes have me drive the tractor pulling the trailer with the grape boxes. Those are Muskat grapes and they pick them to send to a winery for making wine."

Casey said, "Hey, there's somebody a'comin there."
"Oh yeah, that's Don Diego," said Sonny. Don Diego was walking in their direction with a shovel on his shoulder, and as he got closer, he

recognized Sonny and waved. Sonny waved back and shouted, "Hello, Don Diego."

Don is a title that was reserved by people as respect for a man of prominence and usually one who owns property. Don Diego and his brother Alberto had acquired the land several years ago in a trade and farmed it with grapes and fruit trees, and raised some livestock like a few pigs and chickens. They had originally owned the land west of the tracks, but an oil company traded them for the land that they owned where Don Diego's property now stood.

A few years later, Don Diego and Alberto hired a well drilling company to drill for a water well on the property. They were surprised when the water spouted out looking dirty but smelling like oil or gas. What caused that? Everyone wondered for several for months, maybe years later.

As Don Diego approached the fence, Sonny stood up, smiled, and said to Don Diego, "*Buenos dias*, Don Diego."

"*Muy buenos dias*, Sonny," Don Diego responded in his soft quiet voice. Then he said smiling, "I have good news."

"Oh, what's the good news?" Sonny asked.

"My daughter Severina had a new baby this morning. It's good news because *this* baby lived and it's a grandson," Don Diego said.

"That *is* good news," Sonny said. Sonny felt a warm flutter in his heart because he personally loved children and the birth of any child was good cause to celebrate life anywhere and anytime.

"What did they name your new grandson, Don Diego?" Sonny asked.

"I don't know, yet" Don Diego answered. "I will let you know when I find out, if you are still here."

"This time, I will be around for two or three months," Sonny answered. "I am going to be around to help you with the grapes again, Don Diego."

"Good," Don Diego responded, looking around. "We will need help because it looks good this year."

Like most hobos, Sonny did different jobs to earn a living. They were always temporary, but they were jobs, and sometimes the people who hired them got to know the hobos pretty well. Don Diego got to know Sonny as a friend who wasn't always around. But when he was, he was always helping him when needed. They either worked together or Sonny would work alone irrigating, weeding, or driving the tractor to plow or disc.

After Don Diego left, Casey asked Sonny, "So, you're gonna work for him?"

"Yeah, I am," Sonny responded. "Why are you asking?" Sonny asked. "He's my friend and I always help him out whenever I'm in town. His family treats me good, too. They sometimes bring me food out here, or if I'm working on the ranch, I eat under one of the trees or in their backyard. I love Mexican food. I like Don Diego's family, too. They come over and talk to me sometimes."

"Well," Casey said. "In Texas, ah never seen a white man work for a Mexican. The boss always has Mexicans work for him."

"Oh, well this isn't Texas," Sonny responded. "I personally don't see anything wrong with it. Do you?" Sonny asked.

"Hey," Casey said. "There's somebody a'comin yonder." He nodded to the north to where someone was coming toward them along the side of the tracks.

From a distance, the man looked medium-built, but with wide shoulders and walked with a sway, sort of like a sailor. As he got closer, Sonny and Casey could see that he was wearing some baggy jeans and a loosely fitting long sleeved light blue shirt like Casey's. He was wearing a black hat also, but his was smaller than Casey's and was a little crumpled and looked like a small fisherman's or ship captain's cap.

As the man got even closer, Sonny and Casey could hear him mumbling and humming what sounded like a short story in the form of a jingle, "Yep, Popeye goes here and Popeye goes there, but Popeye don't quit. M-m-m-m. Popeye likes juice, but Popeye don't fight. M-m-m-m. Popeye don't dance, but Popeye works hard. M-m-m-m. Popeye's okay. Popeye's happy today."

Sonny just looked, listened, and then smiled. Then he said, "That's Popeye, Casey. He's not crazy even though some say he is, but he's good people. A good man to have around when there's hard work to be done and a need for good company."

"What's the good word, Popeye?" Sonny asked, as he shook hands with Popeye.

Popeye responded with, "Aye, mate. Popeye's just gettin' in from the 'Sheriff's hotel,' Sonny. How are you? Are you feeling the heat yet? Are you gonna stick around for the grapes? Who's your friend?"

Sonny seemed to have forgotten about Casey because Popeye always interested him like he would anyone. "Oh!" said Sonny. "Sorry about the introductions. This is Casey. Just met him today."

"Yesterday, today, or tomorrow, it' always good to meet a new guy out here. Just like out at sea," said Popeye. He shook hands with Casey. "Good to meet ya, mate."

Casey shook hands with Popeye and noticed that he had one eye that was half closed and looked like it had been damaged in an accident. His face was shaven clean but his hair that showed under his hat looked a little long and it was "coal black" in color. He had a light skin color that almost looked pale, and a large nose that kind of looked crooked like a boxer's. His good eye was dark in color, but it seemed to have a "gleam" in it that helped make the face look friendly and warm.

Although Popeye's real name was John, he had been nicknamed "Popeye" because he resembled the cartoon character "Popeye the Sailor Man," the spinach-eating sailor that America had learned to love since early 1929. However, Popeye was a real sailor. He often said, "Aye, mate. Once a sailor, always a sailor." He had worked as a fisherman and worked other odd jobs, on fishing boats and docks along the coast of California around Long Beach, San Pedro, and Morro Bay. He liked to tell sea stories, especially around a fire at night. But when he had had a little "juice" in him, his stories got even more exciting and animated. He told "made up" stories, ghost stories, and many kinds of adventure stories that could even keep the devil himself interested. He was really good at making up and telling his own "parables" based on Bible proverbs. He also had a special story that he told often about a giant whale that almost ate him alive off a small boat that he was in. "Aye, mate. Once upon a time in a storm. Ugliest big fish I ever saw with the biggest tongue and teeth that I will never forget," he would say. Most people didn't take him seriously, but

Sonny did because he believed in Popeye. He always thought that if his own life was ever in danger, Popeye would be there to save him no matter what or no matter when. He was always a good man, a good friend, and a good human being.

Popeye happened to be half Indian Cherokee and half Mexican, and spoke Spanish as well as English. He would say, "I don't know which half is Indian and which half is Mexican. I just feel like an American." Popeye was very patriotic and had been very disappointed when he was rejected by the Army for "flat feet." He never had a problem with people of different "color" or "belief," and was always fair in the treatment of his fellow man. "Aye, mate. Forgive but don't forget. Give a guy a chance if he don't dance, and treat him right with all your might," he would say.

Popeye was not very formally educated, although he was known to read books sometimes. As a child, he went to schools in Hanford, Laton, and Lemoore, and was now known to be somewhat of a self-taught poet and philosopher. Sonny especially liked him for these qualities and that's why he liked him as a good companion. They would engage in discussions about almost everything, especially topics about history, life experiences, travel, and family life. He had family in the Corcoran and Hanford areas, but he very seldom made contact with them except for his sister Sarah who was an ex-nun. The rest of his family shunned him because *they* saw him as "a bum and drunk."

Popeye had been jailed a few times for "public intoxication," but was otherwise a law-abiding citizen and a God-loving soul. He would sometimes go to a Catholic church wherever he was and go in, go up to the altar, kneel, look up at the large crucifix with Jesus, and with a "sheepish" look on his face, make his own "confession in front of God." He didn't really have a lot of sin, but *he* thought that he did. And that's all that mattered. Before he left, he would drop a few coins in the "poor box," dip his fingers in the holy water cup, make the "Sign of the Cross," and leave whistling like he had just "wiped the slate clean," or like a little boy who had just received his first Holy Communion.

Popeye had once told Sonny "in secret" that he had never married because he could never be a "daddy" because of some childhood illness or defect. Possibly, it was caused by the fact that his father used drugs and alcohol heavily when he was young. The doctor had told his mother that he would grow up without being able to father children. He nevertheless loved children. He decided early in life that he would "share" God's children and even those who had "biological parents." Every child then would be a part his family of children.

Because of his "condition," becoming a Catholic priest had entered Popeye's mind when he was a young man. His sister Sarah had already entered a convent then and that inspired him. However, he prayed to Jesus for a "miracle" that could cure him and change his "condition," and then maybe he could become a family man. That stopped him, and so he went on through his young life hoping and praying that it would happen. He worked hard to make money, and again and again, he went to doctors when he could afford it. They all told him the same, "No change." For Popeye, it got be hopeless and he finally gave up and started to roam. No more "secure jobs" and no more "home." His "home" became where he chose to "lay his head" at night.

"Living the life of a hobo isn't so bad 'as long as you keep good company,'" some would say. It is a life where, if you get to know someone, you take care of each other and it's understood, just like a partnership. Sharing food, shelter, stories, or whatever you have to offer is always welcomed. Sometimes hobos would bring someone "home" that they just met to share in whatever the group had like they do at the "hobo jungle." If anyone causes trouble and there are some who do, they are told right away that they need to "get back in line, or git."

After a few minutes of talking among them, Casey blurted out, "Where ya from, Popeye, and what nationality are ya?"

"I'm half Indian and half Mexican, and I'm from around these here parts," Popeye answered.

"Indian?" Casey asked. "Have you ever scalped anybody?"

That more than caught Sonny's attention, and he spoke up, "Hey listen, Casey. That was uncalled for. You need to apologize."

"Nay, no problem, Sonny. He's probably just jokin'," Popeye was quick to say.

"Yeah, ah was jus' jokin," Casey said.

Sonny then said with a little concern in his voice, "Say, listen Casey. Are you moving on?"

"Well, ah was hopin' ah could stay around here and see about pickin' some peaches and makin' some good money."

"Well, Casey," said Sonny. "You can stay for now, but you have to be respectful. Otherwise, some of us around here might not take a liking to you and then you're going to have to leave. Is that clear?"

"Yeah, okay, Sonny," Casey responded.

Popeye didn't say anything because he knew that Sonny was offended by Casey asking what he did and thereby offending *him,* and Sonny didn't really care for people like that. He knows that Sonny is an outspoken person when it comes to those sort of matters, and standing up for people was Sonny's most noticeable and proven quality of character as a person.

Sonny now had a little "group" and thought that it might be a good idea now to go to the "hobo jungle" and see who's around. "Hey, fellas," he then said. "Wanna go over to the "hobo jungle" and see if we could find some of the fellas that I know? Maybe you could find somebody there that knows about the peach picking jobs, Casey."

Popeye looked at Sonny with a frown on his face.

"Yeah, I told him about the heat and fuzz, but he already knew," Sonny responded to Popeye's look.

Sonny was hoping that Casey could find a peach picking job and stay over there because he already felt that he might not like this "new guy." *Well,* he thought to himself. *I just hope that he doesn't offend anybody else over at the "hobo jungle." They just might run us all off.*

All three got up and they started walking north along the tracks to the "hobo jungle." The heat was starting to get more intense. The sun was very bright now and the sky was a bright blue. It appeared to be a beautiful day for some outdoor "socializing" as long as they stayed in the shade. Sonny thought that they should stop at one of the grocery stores and pick up something to "contribute" at the "hobo jungle." He always thought that taking something to share was a symbol of peace, goodwill, and harmony.

At the store, while Casey and Popeye waited outside, Sonny bought some more crackers and some bars of chocolate for boiling with water to drink since no coffee was available now. As he walked up to the counter, he heard on a radio in the store something about the government testing some new weapons, explosives, or bombs. But the newsman wasn't sure what it was since it just seemed to be a rumor. Sonny thought that it may not be a rumor and that maybe something was "brewing" but someone might have "leaked it out." That wasn't uncommon because Sonny had heard, not knowing if it was true, that spies were everywhere in the United States and some "top secrets" had been exposed during the war by spies. *Well, maybe it will all come out soon, or maybe it was just another rumor,* Sonny thought.

They arrived at the "hobo jungle" just in time to see that there were some Sheriff's deputies walking through the "hobo jungle" and among the hobos. As Sonny, Casey, and Popeye walked up, they heard one of the deputies ask the others, "Well, which one?" One of the other deputies pointed to a small young Negro man standing with an old beat up cane, and said, "That one. He looks like a crook." Sonny looked at the young Negro and a "warm flutter" in his heart and a frightful feeling both came over him.

As the incident became tense, Popeye muttered something in a low voice and then Sonny, without even thinking anymore, blurted out, "No, sir, Deputy." Being very careful to seem respectful, he continued, "He's with me and he's been with me since this morning and I just left to get a few 'vittles.' He's just a young man looking for work."

"Who are you? Where have I seen you before?" the deputy, who appeared to be in charge, asked.

"I don't think you have seen me anywhere, sir," Sonny answered, being careful not to give him his name. To the authorities, hobos' names weren't important anyway. Usually, they were people who were here today and gone tomorrow. Sonny then quickly said, "We just got into town this morning, sir."

"Hmm," the deputy said and tried to get a better look at Sonny. Then he said, "Alright, maybe I've never seen you before. But if I have, and if I should remember, we'll be back for you."

Then he said laughing, "Nah, let's not take this one. He looks too skinny. He might eat too much and cost the taxpayers too much money. Take that one over there," he said, pointing to a portly hobo who looked like had he been drinking. Sonny recognized him as Bruto who wasn't too friendly, was somewhat of a bully, and had a loud mouth especially when he had been drinking. He had, in the past, been "banned" from the "hobo jungle" for urinating in front of children. He was reported by the group, but the authorities never came for him. Maybe this was a delayed "time" for him. Surely now, he should have stayed away, so Sonny didn't feel bad about the "unofficial trade."

No one really knew much about Sonny and no really asked him, but Sonny actually was running from the law. Back in a small town in Oklahoma, he had been a Baptist minister by the name of Rev. Silas Andrews. He was a Christian with deep faith and a genuine love for his brothers and sisters in Christ. That's what got him in trouble with law.

Rev. Andrews had helped two Negroes escape from a "chain gang." The two prisoners had been accused of raping a white woman. Sonny knew the truth and knew that they had been framed to protect two men who were members of a white supremacist group and friends of the local police chief.

When the police chief and the group found out that Rev. Andrews was the one who had set the prisoners free, they wanted to hang him. A member of his congregation quickly alerted him and he managed to leave town and Oklahoma. He chose to go as far west as he could manage and chose to go by "Sonny."

After the deputies left, Sonny went over to the young man, asked him his name, and asked if he was okay. The poor fella was trembling and stuttered, "Th-thank you, s-sir. G-God bless you, sir."

"Well, I couldn't see a young man like you going to that jail," Sonny responded. "So what is your name?" he asked again.

"Oh, sorry!" the young man said. "My name . . . My name is Willie. Willie Williams and I'm from Kentucky."

"Okay, Willie," Sonny said. "Are you staying here tonight or got any place to stay?"

"No," Willie said. "I don't know anybody here and I just got here from Bakersfield. I came through Fresno the other day, but I fell asleep on the 'car.'" He was referring to the box car that he had been riding in. "And I went on to Bakersfield, but there was a guy there who told me there are no horse ranches there where I could work. You see, I worked with horses in Kentucky, but they let me go after I got hurt."

"Well," Sonny said. "I don't know if there are any horse ranches for you to work on around here either, but we could ask around. If nothing turns up for you, we can look for other work together."

"Oh! That would be very kind of you, sir," Willie responded.

After spending some time with other hobos and "socializing" until it was getting dark, Sonny, Popeye, Casey, and Willie were leaving together, when a man was arriving at the "hobo jungle."

"Hey Sonny! Hey Popeye," he called out.

"Hey, Slim," Sonny responded. "How's it going for you?"

"I'm real okay," Slim answered and shook hands with Sonny. "I've been working for a man digging ditches and laying pipe."

"Sounds like a good job, Slim. Does he need any more help?"

"Yeah," Slim said. "He asked me today if I knew anymore 'good men' like me. I told him I would look around for him and let him know. He said to just bring them over in the morning for him to take a look at. Are you guys interested?"

"Yeah," said Sonny. "We are all interested, right men?" He asked as he looked around at the group.

They all answered, "Right!"

The group walked back to Sonny's camp and there was a bit of chatter. "Well, ah guess the peaches can wait," said Casey. "If we got a job tomorrow."

"Yeah, if what Jim said back at the 'jungle.' The peaches are still a little green right now, anyway. You might as well dig some ditches with Slim, too. We can probably all work good as a team," said Sonny.

"Yeah, but what about this kid?" asked Casey.

"What do you mean?" Sonny asked Casey.

"Well, you know, he looks too young and he's colored," said Casey.

"Look, Casey!" said Sonny, with his impatience starting to show. "I thought that you understood about being respectful?"

"Okay, okay," said Casey. "But what about his age and his bad leg?"

Sonny turned to Willie, and asked, "If you don't mind if I ask, how old are you Willie?"

"I'm sixteen, Mr. Sonny," Willie answered.

"Well, you are pretty young after all," Sonny responded. "I guess we'll have to look after you."

Casey did not say anything, but Sonny already could feel *his* problem with having to look after Willie, so he said, "I will look after him."

"Aye, me, too!" Popeye spoke up.

"Okay, thanks," Sonny told Popeye. "*We* will look out for him."

Willie must have felt like he was already a burden, so he offered his "peace," too, "I won't be no trouble Mr. Casey and Mr. Sonny and Mr. Popeye, I can look out for myself. I have been on my own for a few months now and I have been doing okay. I can cook, too. After my job at the horse ranch, I cooked at a diner and I was doing good except the owner died and the family had to close up."

It was starting to get dark. As the group walked along the tracks past Fourth Street, a little boy was playing near the tracks. "Hey, Carlito," called Sonny waving to him. "You should go home now. It's getting dark." Carlito just smiled. Sonny and Popeye already knew Carlito, so Sonny said to Willie and Casey, "Carlito's deaf and he doesn't talk."

Casey said, "Oh, you mean deaf and dumb?"

"No, not dumb," said Sonny sternly. "He's a really smart child and a good boy. He's only four, but he knows a lot more than most children his age. His mother and grandmother are raising him. His father was killed in France in the war two years ago."

As Carlito started to walk away, he suddenly looked up and pointed toward the sky.

"Hey, look," said Popeye. "Two shooting stars."

"Praise the Lord," Willie said softly. The others just watched as the two shooting stars streaked across the quickly darkening sky. Then they just seemed to go faster and then they fizzled out softly in a cloud of mist as if some sort of energy was released.

No one spoke as the group walked along the tracks back to the camp. Then, Casey asked jokingly, "Well, did y'all make a wish?"

Popeye answered, "Aye, once when I was a kid, I made a wish that my dog would come back because we couldn't find him. But he never did come back. Then when I was older, my grandfather told me that a car killed him and they buried him without telling me. I never forgot that dog. Never had one like him again either. Maybe he was a mongrel, an alley dog you know. But to me, he was the best dog in the whole wide world. Whenever anybody came near me and my sister Sarah, he would growl at them. But that just happened with me and my sister because he hardly ever barked at anybody."

"Well, ah never believe in that stuff mah self," said Casey. "Ah just figure, if ya got good luck ya do, and if ya got bad luck, too bad. Mah'self, ah got nothin' but bad luck. That's why I left Texas. Mah wife shot me in the leg and the cop took *me* in 'cause he was her cousin. When ah got outta the pokey, ah decided it's time to git and here ah am. Maybe ah'll have better luck out here."

As the group got to the campsite, Willie spoke, "Well, I don't know about making a wish on shooting stars, but my grandma said that they are souls going straight to heaven."

Casey looked at him and said, "Ya'll believe in that?"

"Yes, sir, Mr. Casey," Willie responded.

"Hmph," Casey mumbled.

Popeye then spoke up, "I'll go for that, Willie. It sounds like real good belief. Only God really knows, but you just hang on to that Willie."

Just then, a shower of shooting stars streaked across the sky and the group of men looked up in amazement. Sonny said excitedly, "Will you look at that? I have never seen anything like that. I wonder what's going on?"

Willie said, "Maybe it's because of the war. Maybe a lot of people got killed today."

Then Popeye spoke up, "Yeah, maybe so. My cousin Freddy was killed a year ago in France, and my cousin James was killed in England two years ago. Then my friend's son was killed last year somewhere in Europe. I hope that war will end soon."

Just as Popeye said that, another shower of shooting stars went over them. "Ooh!" they all said at the same time.

Sonny said, "Maybe Willie's right. Maybe it has something to do with the war. Must be a big battle going on somewhere."

"Aw, ya'll not going to believe that, too, are ya?" Casey quipped.

"Well," said Sonny. "I know that it gives me goose bumps just standing here looking at this show."

Casey started to complain about his wounded leg. Willie asked him, "Can I massage your leg for you Mr. Casey?"

Casey looked at him and started to say something with a sarcastic look on his face. Sonny interrupted him with, "Casey!"

Casey then apparently changed his mind and said to Willie, "Well, what do know about massaging a leg?"

"Well," Willie responded apologetically. "I know you're not a horse, but I massaged a lot of horses' legs back in Kentucky when I worked on the horse ranch, and I even did that for my friends and family."

"Well, okay," said Casey. "Let's give 'er a try."

Willie looked at Sonny, and Sonny nodded to him. Willie pulled out some liniment out of his bag and asked Casey to roll up his pants leg. "This will hurt a little at first, Mr. Casey, but it will get better," he assured Casey.

As Willie started, Casey let out a loud grunt and showed pain on his face. As the massage progressed, Casey's face turned calmer. Willie asked him, "Is it getting better, Mr. Casey?"

"Yeah," Casey answered. "It feels good. Hey! How come you don't talk like other colored people?"

"Well," Willie answers. "I was raised by white people and I went to school, too. And I like to read sometimes."

Willie finished massaging Casey's leg, and Casey thanked him. They all went to bed that night looking up at the sky, as more showers of shooting stars silently streamed across the sky. No one said anything, but soon the camp was full with soft snoring as if the star show in the dark sky seemed to have some pacifying effect on the group of men. The show continued for about an hour or more with periodic spurts lighting the sky as if a celebration was taking place.

The next day, the group got up early and after some "good mornings," they cooked some breakfast. Popeye took on the job of making coffee out of some left over grounds that Casey was carrying. The coffee soon filled the air with the all too familiar aroma. Sonny pulled out some crackers and a can of sardines, and Willie pulled out some corn bread wrapped in a package made of cheese cloth. Casey pulled out some dried meat that almost looked like tobacco because of its dark color and rough texture.

As the men ate and shared the food and enjoyed their breakfast, the sun was beginning to rise to the east. The sunrise served as bright reddish-orange colored background for the dark Sierra-Nevada Mountains, as they in turn served as a majestically tall rough and jagged dark wall that helped enclose the vast San Joaquin Valley. The air was cool and soon the noise of automobiles carrying people to work could be heard. And in the neighborhood, the aroma of fresh-made tortillas, fried bacon, and chorizo; softly filled the air along with an accent of freshly brewing coffee.

"Well, mates, I guess my people are up," said Popeye with a chuckle. "Sure is good to be out in the free world again, especially in this neighborhood."

"Well," said Sonny. "I hope you'll stay around for a while and help with the grapes."

"Aye, mate, I aim to stay out of trouble," said Popeye, with a commitment in his voice.

Popeye was known to get in trouble from time to time, but it wasn't for anything that he did to anyone. It was always the "juice" that got him in trouble. "Being drunk in public," as the judges around here called it, was not tolerated especially around the downtown area. Popeye sometimes wandered there "just to see what was going on." One time, the police found him next to the large fountain in front of the Civic Auditorium. He just had to have a drink of water at one of the spigots, but he passed out after sipping a little water. He later woke up across the street in the Kings County Jail.

That incident cost Popeye more than the usual time in jail, because the park in front of the Civic Auditorium was where many families would go to after a visit to Superior Dairy across the street for ice cream. They would bring their treats to the park and sit and enjoy a family time. Popeye didn't ever mean to spoil anyone's good time especially a family time, but no one knew that. When he sobered up and realized what he did, he felt ashamed of himself and vowed to make sure never to wander over there again.

As the group finished their breakfast, Sonny spoke up, "Say, men. If we're going to have a job today, we'd better get going. Slim might start thinking that we might not be interested."

"Well, 'am mighty interested," said Casey. "Ah'm almost broke and need some money to get around. Maybe then I can get out and pick some peaches."

"Maybe I can go, too, Mr. Casey," said Willie and looked for an approval.

"Well, ah don't know. With that limp of yours and my limp, they might think they don't want to hire two cripples 'stead o' just one."

"Well," Willie responded. "I don't want you to be any trouble, but I would sure like to taste some of them sweet ripe peaches."

"Yeah," said Sonny. "Maybe you can bring him some, Casey. After all, he helped you with your leg."

"Well, we'll see about that," said Casey.

As the group traveled north along the tracks, they could hear a train coming in the distance. More people were up now. Probably because it was starting to get hot, some kids were already up, too. As they passed Third Street and approached Fourth Street, they spotted Carlito. He was playing on top of the tracks, jumping from board to board like in some kind of skipping game. Forgetting for a moment that Carlito was deaf, Sonny shouted to him, "Hey, Carlito, get off those tracks. A train's coming." Of course, Carlito didn't hear him and so he did not move off the tracks. Sonny jogged over to him and grabbed him from the waist and carried him down away from the tracks and pointed to the train that was now nearing Sixth Street. Carlito looked at Sonny, smiled, and gave him a "thumbs up," then he ran off to play with a dog nearby. Carlito didn't always play with other children. It was probably because of his handicap and it was probably no fun to not being able to talk, laugh, and play with them. He made up his own games and seemed to have fun all by himself.

Sonny and his group got to Sixth Street where Slim and a husky man were standing. Slim waved to the group and as they neared the two men.

Slim said to the other man, "These are the men I was telling you about, Mr. Roberts." Sonny glanced at Mr. Roberts as if to quickly study him to see if he could tell what type of man he was. Sonny was always doing that because he always wanted to make sure that he wasn't going to have any problems with anyone, and now he had a group of men that he felt responsible for.

Slim introduced Sonny first, and then Sonny introduced each man.

Mr. Roberts then asked, "What about him?" He nodded to Willie.

"Well, sir," said Sonny, almost sounding defensive and protective of Willie. "He needs a job just like anybody else, and can do a job like any white man can."

"Well," Mr. Roberts quickly responded. "I didn't mean anything like that Sonny. I am just wondering how old he is."

Willie quickly spoke up, wanting to be honest and of no problem to Sonny and the other men, "I'm sixteen, sir, but I have been on my own now for a few months and I have done many different jobs and I can work hard, sir."

Sonny had already been surprised at Willie's age, so now he quickly spoke up, "I'll take responsibility for him, Mr. Roberts. I'll make sure that we don't have any problems."

"Aye, sir. Me, too," spoke up Popeye in support of Sonny's commitment. Casey didn't say anything but had a resentful look on his face as was now starting to become usual when it came to Willie.

Mr. Roberts said to the group of men, "Well, I have to go over to Redington Street to get another crew going. Slim will tell you men what to do and he'll keep your time. You'll get paid at the end of the day at forty-five cents an hour because this is hard work. Quittin' time is three o'clock because it gets too hot after that. Don't want anybody getting too sick. Oh, and by the way, I'll get somebody to bring out some drinking water for you, men."

Casey spoke up, "Thank you very much, Mr. Roberts. That's mighty kind of you to pay us at the end of the day 'cause ah sure need that."

Sonny now begin to feel better about Mr. Roberts, and he decided that even though it was only a few minutes, Mr. Roberts came across as a fair and decent man. As Mr. Roberts walked away, Popeye smiled and said, "I like him. This might be hard work, but I think I'm going to like it."

"Me, too," quipped Willie.

Casey agreed and Sonny made it unanimous.

Slim showed the men what they were to do. It was digging ditches, but they had to be jumping in and out of the ditches as they dug then pitched dirt out of the newly dug ditch. As time passed, the men were starting to understand what Mr. Roberts meant when he said hard work. This was work that caused calluses on men's already rough hands and soreness on men's already sore backs from sleeping on the ground. With the sun bearing down on them, sweat pouring out on their faces, and dirt turning into mud on those sweating faces, it was now turning the men into what looked like wet dogs who had been in the swamp near the oil refinery on Third Street.

It was now afternoon. Willie didn't seem to be having any trouble with his leg, but Casey was now starting to have trouble with his. He was in pain and it showed on his face. Sonny was the first to notice, and so he said, "Hold it, men. Let's take a break."

As they leaned on the fresh dirt inside of the ditch, Sonny decided that something had to be done and suggested, "How about if we take turns with two of us digging and two of us pitching the dirt further away from the ditch and then we can pile it up later and we won't have to all be climbing in and out?"

"Okay," said Popeye. "That sounds good."

"Want me to massage your leg later, Mr. Casey?" asked Willie.

"Yeah. Thanks, Willie," Casey answered, sounding friendlier toward Willie than he ever did.

Sonny listened to Casey's and Willie's conversation, and within himself felt a good thing coming. He thought to himself how sometimes men facing the same odds under trying circumstances could smooth out differences between them no matter who they were and how they felt.

"How are you doing?" he then asked Popeye, as if to add to the brotherhood already developing among them. Popeye answered smiling, "I'm okay, mate. I think I'll live. It will take more than ditch digging to kill an Indian-Mexican."

As three o'clock rolled around, Slim arrived in his beat up pickup and got out with a cloth bag, a piece of paper, and a pencil. "Well," he said. "It's quitting time and payday, too." He opened the bag and counted out each man's pay and wrote on the paper. "Well, are you all coming back in the morning?" he asked.

"Yeah," they all answered.

As they began to leave, the group saw a short train pass, but it was going a little faster than usual because it was only pulling a few cars. As they walked a little further, Willie said to Casey, "Yes, sir, Mr. Casey. I'll tend to that leg as soon as we get back."

"Thanks, Willie," Casey responded, walking with obvious pain. Just then, the group heard three long blasts of a train horn.

"Wonder what happened," said Sonny. "That usually means that the train either hit a car or somebody."

Suddenly, Sonny and Popeye quickly turned to each other with the look of horror in their faces and said at the same time, "Carlito!"

Sonny and Popeye started to run in the direction of a crowd of people on the tracks. The train was stopped on the tracks some distance from the crowd of people. Sonny and Popeye could hear some women crying, and one was screaming and moaning in Spanish, "Carlito, Carlito, *Dios mio*!"

Sonny's heart sank and it started beating fast. He was hoping and praying to God that it wasn't so and that he would see Carlito standing nearby. As he approached closely, he saw Carlito's small body lying on the side of tracks where the train apparently threw him on impact. Sonny's eyes were now watery and he started to shake in disbelief. Then as he wiped his tears, he looked up the tracks. Standing a short distance away, he saw Carlito who smiled and waved at him. But then he disappeared as fast as he appeared. Sonny immediately and sadly knew what that meant, and he waved to the spot where he saw Carlito standing.

Popeye saw what Sonny did, but did not say anything. He pretty much had an idea what Sonny was doing. Popeye then lifted his hand and also waved slowly at the spot that Sonny waved at. With tears in his eyes, he thought about Carlito and how much he and Sonny were going to miss him. Carlito's smile was enough to make anyone feel good. Liking and caring about Carlito was easy, but what was hard was to accept that the lovable child was now gone. Popeye thought to himself, *Aye, if God took Carlito, then it was for a good reason and no one should question it. Such things always happen for a reason and usually that would be known if people would just pay enough attention. We go through life doing what we have to do for the day and every day, but we don't stop often enough to think about what is really going on around us. We miss the lessons in life that are important. Children are important, but too often, we forget that they are there and why they are there, and then we forget to watch and protect them. When something like this happens, we usually think about what the child could have been, but we don't think about what they were and don't spend enough time to get to know them to realize who they really were.*

As the group walked past the accident scene to their camp, the men did not say anything at first. Then, Willie spoke up, "God bless, Carlito's momma. She will miss him forever, but I hope that she can understand soon that he's with God now."

Then Sonny finally spoke, "Well, it will be a long time for her to understand that I'm sure. Losing a child like that is probably the worst thing that can happen to a mother."

Popeye also spoke, "Aye, mates. I'll go to the church tomorrow and pray for her and her family and light a candle for Carlito. If anyone wants to go with me, you are welcome to come. You don't have to be Catholic, you know."

Then Casey said, "I don't know what I could do. I don't go to church, but I feel bad for the mother."

That night, as the group settled down to have their dinner, they sat around quietly and it was apparent that sadness had taken over the camp. Then, Popeye looked up and said, "Look mates, a little shooting star!"

"Praise the Lord," whispered Willie. "Go, Carlito, go."

Sonny looked up, too, and then he shouted, "Yeah! Go, Carlito, go!"

Casey looked at them with a surprised look on his face, but said nothing. Then he looked down and just shook his head.

The little shooting star was traveling fast, but it also seemed to have a special brightness to it. It suddenly slowed down and curved down slightly. Then, a bright shower of its lighted pieces scattered as if to signify a symbol of spreading Carlito's ashes in the dark sky among the bigger stars. Anyone who saw this certain spectacular event and understood Willie's beliefs would say that Carlito was now at peace in Heaven.

The next day after breakfast, Sonny, Popeye, and Willie went back to work at the ditch digging job. Casey went to the "hobo jungle" to see if he could find out if anyone knew where he could find a peach picking job.

Casey arrived at the "hobo jungle" and found a few men there. Casey didn't waste any time asking around for information. Ralph, a short man with a beard, told Casey that if he went over to Fifth Street and waited in front of a small bar there, a truck would come out every hour to pick up people who wanted to work picking peaches. The peaches were ripening quickly now because of the hot weather, and the ranchers needed to harvest the crops quickly and so they needed more pickers.

Casey quickly started walking to Fifth Street. As he got to the bar that Ralph had told him about, he noticed that there were only two men there. As he approached them, Casey called out, "Am I too late for the peach picking ride?"

"No," a small man with a large brimmed hat and a slight Spanish accent called out. "They didn't have enough room for us so they'll be back."

"Good," said Casey. "Ah thought ah missed out."

As Casey leaned up and waited along the wall of the bar, he thought about the work that was going to finally be ahead of him. The heat and fuzz might to too much for him, but at least he would try it. Hard work didn't bother him too much, but he was wondering about who was going to be his boss. He then started to think that maybe he should have stayed with Sonny and the rest of the group. Slim and Mr. Roberts were okay.

The truck soon arrived and the driver shouted to them, "Y'all going to the Murray Ranch on Thirteenth Avenue?"

"Yeah," they all answered.

"Okay, then. Jump in 'cause you're losing time to make some money."

As the rickety truck sped out of town into the country, the three men sat silently and held on to their hats as the wind rush passed them. Then Casey spoke, half shouting, "Well, this is mah first time pickin' peaches. How's the work?"

One of the men responded, "Well, it's hot and the fuzz gets bad, but if you work hard and fast, you forget about it. Then, at the end of the day, you can get a good handful of money. It's not forever. The grapes come after the peaches."

"Yeah, I know," said Casey. "But is the boss a good man?"

"The boss comes out to check on the crew sometimes, but he has a foreman named Don Diego. Don Diego has his own ranch, but he comes to help this rancher out when the peaches are ready to pick."

"Oh, ah know Don Diego," said Casey.

"Then you know that he's a good man," the man said. "Yeah, ah don't know him too good, but Sonny knows him more and he says that Don Diego is a good man."

As the truck arrived at the ranch, Casey could see that pickers were already at work in the orchards. Some workers were on ladders picking peaches off the trees and others were walking around the trunks of trees picking the peaches that were hanging from the lower branches. The sound of peaches being dropped into the metal buckets was something Casey had never heard before. This was a totally different experience for him.

Casey and the other two men were directed to a man standing near two stacks of wooden boxes and a pile of buckets. One stack of boxes was neatly piled in rows with freshly picked peaches in them. The other stack was empty boxes ready to be filled. The man was holding a large booklet and appeared to be taking down a count as the pickers dumped their buckets of picked peaches in the boxes. The sweet aroma of freshly picked peaches was in the air and voices of pickers could be heard as they worked. The conversations seemed to be about anything and some were in Spanish. The pickers worked fast using two buckets each, and after dumping their filled buckets, almost ran back to their ladders which they quickly scampered up to start picking again.

Casey spotted Don Diego walking between the rows of peach trees and seemed to be supervising the crew as he pointed to some missed branches with peaches. When he looked in Casey's direction, Casey waved at him but Don Diego did not seem to recognize Casey. Casey shouted, "I stay with Sonny by the tracks near your ranch."

Don Diego nodded but did not say anything. Then Don Diego motioned to the man near the boxes and said "okay" while pointing to Casey. To Casey, this meant he had a job because the man picked up two buckets and handed them to Casey. Then he told Casey, "Get a ladder over there. Get a twelve-foot one. The trees aren't too tall here. Then, start on that tree". He pointed to a peach tree along the dirt road where the crew was working.

Casey carried his buckets to the tree, and then went and got a ladder. Since he had never worked at picking peaches, he watched the other pickers as he carried the ladder to the tree. He immediately decided that this was not going to be easy if he was going to make any money being that it was ten cents a box which took two buckets to fill. Then he remembered about the heat and fuzz, which was not even a problem yet.

Casey decided that he would at least give it a try, and if it was too much for him, then it would be back to ditch digging with Sonny and the rest of his group. He started to pick and to help himself mentally and started to softly whistle a tune that didn't even have a name. However, that whistling came to a quick stop when he encountered a wasp nest and was stung on the hand as he tried to swat off the wasps as they attacked. Quickly going down the ladder, he shook his hand in pain. He then felt a hand on his shoulder. It was Don Diego. He handed him a newspaper wrapped like a funnel and some matches. "Burn them," Don Diego told him. Casey looked at the paper and matches and then looked up at the wasp nest where the wasps had settled again. Don Diego knew then that he had to show Casey how to handle the wasps, so he took the paper and lit it with a match. He then took his hat off and climbed the ladder with the lit "torch" and moved up until he got close enough to the nest and shoved it up there. Of course he didn't burn all of the wasps because some flew off, but it was enough for Casey to get back up to pick peaches again. Don Diego then climbed back down the ladder and told Casey to go to the drinking water container and to get water and dirt to make some mud to put on his hand where he was stung Then, he quietly walked away to resume his supervisory duties.

For Casey, the morning seemed to never end. His leg was bothering him and the fuzz from the peaches was starting to penetrate his skin with an intense itch that he had never felt before. He remembered what Sonny had said about him possibly being allergic to the fuzz. So far, Casey didn't think he was allergic, but he thought that only time would tell. The wasps was something that no one had warned him about, but now it was another thing that he had to worry about because just in this morning, he had encountered two more nests of the demonic creatures. He burned them as Don Diego had shown him to do, but he realized that this had slowed him down. Then Casey wondered what other hazards might exist that no one had warned him about.

Don Diego came around to the tree that Casey was picking on now, and asked him, "Are you okay?"

"Yes, sir, ah'm okay," answered Casey. "Say, Don Diego, could I take a peach or two after the day is over? I have a friend who wants a taste of these little devils?"

"Yes," answered Don Diego, "That will be okay."

Casey thought that Willie would really like that and Sonny would probably like that, too.

Don Diego shouted out, "Twelve o'clock." This meant that it was lunch time, although there was no official time out for lunch. The pickers were really on their own as far as their time was concerned. Many of the men had been taking occasional "breaks" to eat and drink something throughout the morning. This kind of work took a lot of energy, and eating throughout the day was common. In any case, most of the pickers came down from their ladders and sat down in small groups under the trees to eat their lunches. Some had lunch pails and some just had lunch bags of different sorts. Casey pulled out a small bag of some cracker crumbs and some dried meat out of his pockets. Not bringing anything to drink, he would go to the water container for water to wash down his lunch. He thought about eating a peach for dessert, but decided that he did not want to ask Don Diego for one again. He had heard that taking fruit was not something that pickers could do as they pleased, so he did not want to do anything that he felt was forbidden. Don Diego had already been more than kind enough, and he certainly did not want to ruin that and then Sonny finding out about it.

As the day passed, Casey realized that it takes some skill to be a peach picker. Having to be careful to only pick the right peaches was a skill in itself, but he started getting the hang of it. The man taking count gave Casey some guidance, but he could only be so much help. His leg was giving him trouble. Climbing on and off the ladder and the heat and fuzz were taking their toll on him. By the time 4:00 p.m. came around, Casey had only fifteen boxes to his credit. This sounded like a lot of work, but at ten cents a box, that only meant $1.50. Casey thought that his hopes of making a good living at picking peaches were now just that, hopes.

Soon after four o'clock, the first truck drove up to the orchard to pick up the first group of pickers who wanted to call it a day. Casey decided that he wasn't going to be a fool, and so he decided that he was getting on that truck to go home. After he was paid cash for his work that day, he asked Don Diego again if he could take a couple of peaches. Don Diego told him "okay," then pointed to some boxes with peaches that were sorted out as being too ripe for shipping but ripe enough for drying. Casey reached into a box and picked out two peaches and put them into his bag where he had carried his lunch. He could smell the sweet peaches that had quickly ripened in the heat. By now, his bad leg was pretty sore and so he had trouble climbing onto the truck.

As the truck traveled back to town and headed to the bar where the men were picked up, Casey thought about giving Willie the peaches but now he was thinking that maybe everybody was going to want one. "Well" he thought. "If I go back tomorrow, I'll ask Don Diego if I could bring a couple more." For now, he needed to pay back Willie for his leg massaging and that was important because he was sure going to need him tonight.

As the truck arrived at the bar, Casey could hear a noisy crowd inside. Casey thought that it might not hurt to go in and get a shot of whiskey to help with the pain in his leg. One of the other men in the truck said, "I think I'll go in and have a cold beer. Anybody else coming?"

Casey answered, "Yeah, me."

The other men said they were going home to families, so they got off the truck and walked away in different directions.

Once inside the bar, Casey saw a familiar scene. Several men who were dressed in their work clothes were drinking and talking loudly. Some were sitting at the bar and some were sitting around tables or just standing around. A couple of men were playing pool. A jukebox was loudly playing music and some men were talking and laughing with a rather large heavy woman behind the bar who was bartending.

Casey walked up to the bar and motioned to the bartender that he wanted a drink. She came over to where he was and Casey noticed, even in the dim light, that she had heavy makeup covering wrinkles and she had straight black hair. She had a tattoo on her left arm that had a red rose and an inscription that read "Sweet As A Peach." She had a red ribbon on her hair and a front tooth missing. "What's it gonna be, buddy?" she asked Casey.

"A shot of your house whiskey," he answered a little loudly because of the noise in the bar. She momentarily hesitated and seemed to be studying his face which made Casey a little uneasy. Then she said, "Okay." She reached for a bottle of whiskey and a small glass on the shelf behind her that also had a photo of a young man in Army uniform.

She poured the whiskey into the glass, and then asked Casey, "You from Texas or Oklahoma?"

Casey paid for his drink and then said, "Texas. How'd ya know?"

"I know people and I can tell by the way you look and talk. But don't worry, I don't mean anything bad by that," she said. "Besides knowing liquor, part of my business is knowing people. I own this bar and I worry a little about getting people in here who might be trouble. Yeah, Heavy Evie. That's what they call me. Don't want any trouble with anybody. If you just come in here to talk, play pool, or just listen to the music and drink, that's okay. But if you start trouble, you have to git someplace else where they take animals."

Casey nodded uneasily, but he couldn't decide if this was a safe place to have a drink or not. Back in Texas, he frequented bars, but he pretty much knew which ones were okay and which ones were not.

Just as Casey was finishing his drink and was about to leave, a loud argument started between the two guys playing pool. Heavy Evie shouted, "Knock it off, you two, or you gotta git!"

The two continued arguing and suddenly, the smaller of the two and he wasn't that small, swung his cue stick at the other guy, just missing him. Heavy Evie ran around from behind the bar and told them both, "Alright, that's it. You both gotta get out!"

But the bigger guy now suddenly decided to take his turn and swung his cue stick, hitting the other guy in the arm. While some of the others in the bar started to cheer, Heavy Evie, with her left hand, grabbed onto the bigger guy's arm that was holding the cue stick, and with her right fist, punched and landed the blow square on the side of the guy's jaw. That sent him reeling to the floor, and this time, the whole bar crowd cheered loudly. Heavy Evie then turned to the other guy, but with a horrified look on his face, he just dropped his cue stick and ran out the door. This made the crowd go loudly wild with laughter. The other guy was knocked out in the first round, so that event was over. Heavy Evie reached for an almost full glass of beer on a table and splashed it on the knocked-out guy's face. He didn't come to right away, so she reached for him and shook him until he opened his eyes. Upon seeing Heavy Evie, he covered his face and head. Then, Heavy Evie said to him, "Alright, ya bum. Ya lost, so now pick yourself up and get outta here before I pop ya one again and throw ya out myself!"

The guy scrambled up and stumbled out of the bar because he knew that Heavy Evie was serious. Once again, the bar crowd went wild with laughter.

Casey decided that he had had enough excitement and entertainment for the day, so he left the bar. Outside the bar, he saw two police cars arrive. The officers got out of their cars and hurriedly walked up to the bar. Then one asked Casey, "Big fight in there?"

"Not no more," Casey answered. "It's over. Heavy Evie took care of it."

"Oh, okay," the officer said. "Well then, no need to go in there, Bob," he said to the other officer. They got back in their cars and left.

As Casey walked across town toward the campsite at the tracks, he thought about home. He didn't have any children, just an "ex-wife" as far as he was concerned. But he did have his elderly mother and a blind younger brother, and he began to wonder how they were. When he came to California, he thought that he might work and make enough money to send some home. But now that he had tried picking peaches and knew that his bad leg would always give him trouble, he knew that it was going to be hard. Even the ditch digging job he did with Sonny and the others was hard on him, he now began to wonder if he could ever find a job that he could do well. Knowing that he had worked at hard jobs before his injury made him feel helpless. *Maybe*, he thought to himself. *Ah will have to go back to Texas and apply for some kind of welfare*. But the thought of doing that made him think of himself as a "freeloader" and he certainly didn't want anyone else thinking that, too. He decided that he wasn't going to quit so easily.

As he was nearing Phillips Street, he saw Popeye coming in his direction.

"Hey, Casey!" Popeye sounded like he was glad to see Casey.

"Hey, Popeye!" Casey *was* glad to see Popeye.

"Are ya guys done for the day?" Casey asked.

"Aye, mate," said Popeye. "I'm going to my sister's to take a shower. She has a shower and a wash sink outside by the garage. She has a toilet outhouse, too. I use them sometimes when I need to clean up. Wanna go, too? I had asked Sonny and Willie if they wanted to, but they went to the bathhouse on Sixth Street and then they were going to the drug store to get some liniment. Looks like Willie will be busy tonight. He said that he knew that you would need some massaging, and maybe all of us need one."

"That's mighty kind of him," said Casey. "He's a good boy, isn't he?"

Popeye being surprised by Casey's comment, answered, "Uh, yeah. That he is mate."

"Well, I guess ah'll go with you, Popeye. Where does your sister live?" asked Casey.

"Just over there on Third Street across from the refinery," answered Popeye. They started walking, and then Popeye started telling Casey how the day went digging ditches.

"Well, Popeye," Casey said. "My day at picking peaches wasn't too good. Ah had no idea that it was going to be that hard. When you think of sweet peaches, you think of good things. I had my mind set wrong. The heat, the fuzz, the wasps, and my bad leg made it a bad and long day. The only good thing was that Don Diego was there to help me some. I don't know if ah will be goin' back, but ah never was a quitter and ah don't want to be one now. Ah shore don't want to go back to Texas. Nothin' but trouble waits for me there."

"Well," said Popeye. "A man has to look out for himself, but he also has to make up his own mind and be his own boss. It's good for the mind, heart, and soul, you know."

Popeye and Casey arrived at Sarah's house. It was a small house as were most of the houses in the neighborhood. They walked up onto the porch and Popeye knocked. "If she's not home, I just go in back and clean up and then I leave her a note on this pad hanging here. I always let her know that I was here."

Sarah was home and she greeted the two at the door. "Hello, John. Got a friend today?"

"Yeah, Sister," answered Popeye. "This is Casey." Being that she was an ex-nun, Popeye always referred to Sarah as "Sister" or "Sister Sarah," so this was not just because she was his real sister.

Sarah said, "Hello, Casey. I'm glad to meet you."

"Ah'm glad to meet you, too," responded Casey, while taking off his hat.

Popeye then told Sarah, "We're going to clean up in the back, okay?"

"Of course," said Sarah. "And you're both staying for dinner. I'm cooking your favorite John, chili verde, fresh cooked beans, rice, fresh-made salsa, and I just made some tortillas to eat with butter just like you always like."

"Oh, good!" said Popeye. "Well, what do you think Casey?"

"Sounds good to me, if it ain't too much bother," answered Casey.

"It's no bother, Casey. You and my brother are welcome. I'll finish cooking dinner and you men go get cleaned up."

Sarah was a short plump lady with a pleasantly pretty face without any makeup. She had darker colored skin than Popeye's and straight long black hair. She had a soft voice and appeared to be older than Popeye. She was wearing a long flowered dress and wore a large cross on a necklace. Except for her friendly personality, she did not seem to resemble Popeye very much.

As Casey went into the house after he and Popeye cleaned up, he noticed that the walls were lined with hanging family photos, a crucifix, photos of Saints, and a large picture of "Our Lady of Guadalupe." He knew that picture because his friend Humbierto in Texas had a picture something like it in the living room of his home. Humbierto had told Casey that Mexican Catholics consider her sacred, and honor and adore her. Humbierto told Casey that in the early fifteen hundreds, she was the Lady who was an apparition of the Virgin Mary. A Mexican Indian named

Juan Diego reported to the Church that she had appeared and spoke to him on a hill near where Mexico City is now. All Mexican Catholics knew the story in one form or another and celebrated the event annually on December 12, the anniversary of the event.

Casey was not new to Mexican people's culture and heritage, so the aroma of Sarah's cooking coming from the small kitchen was familiar and enticing. *Oh, boy*, he thought to himself. *This is going to be a real treat*. He even temporarily forgot about the pain in his leg. He was now *very* glad that he met up with Popeye.

As the two men sat down at Sarah's table, she placed a large bowl of the hot chili verde on the table. Then, she put plates and forks in front of the men. The basket with fresh tortillas, bowls of hot beans and rice, a bowl of fresh salsa, and a container with butter followed. Sarah joined the two men but first a made the "Sign of the Cross" as Catholics do before a prayer, and said a prayer of thanks for the food. Casey bowed his head, and when Sarah was finished praying, he said "amen," as did Popeye. He had joined in this ritual in Humbierto's home many times. In this certain instance, Casey was comfortable in being respectful and he felt at home. It was just like whenever he visited Humbierto's home. He had always known Mexican families to be hospitable. Sometimes it was overwhelming because they many times went out of their way to make a guest feel welcomed and at home. The saying "*mi casa es su casa*" was not just a figure of speech. Mexican people made sure that a guest felt it.

As they ate, Sarah began the conversation. "This was our parents' house. John and I grew up here with another brother named Matthew and a sister named Mary." Sarah always called people by their Christian names. She rarely referred to her brother as "Popeye." "Our father died three years ago of cancer. It was then that I came home to live with our mother to care for her. But then she died last year of cancer, too." She looked at Popeye and said, "John comes around from time to time and I'm glad because our other brother and sister live out of town. John and I were always close. Weren't we, John?"

"Aye, Sister," said Popeye. "We teamed up for mischief when we were kids. If I got in trouble, Sister would always defend me. But I wasn't that bad was I, Sister?"

"No," Sarah laughed. "You were just a curious little rascal who couldn't resist temptation to find out about everything and everybody."

"Aye," said Popeye with a chuckle. "That, I was."

Casey was impressed with the close relationship between Popeye and his sister Sarah. He then spoke, "Ah had a sister, but she died when she was six. I have two brothers, too, but ah haven't seen one of them for years. Ah think he lives somewhere in eastern Texas, but in what town it is, ah don't know. My family wasn't very close. My mama and daddy split up when ah was eight. Haven't seen my daddy ever since. My youngest brother lives with mah mama. He's blind."

"I am sorry to hear that. Where in Texas are you from?" asked Sarah.

"Sweetwater," answered Casey. "Oh," said Sarah. "I don't know where that is."

"It's in northwestern Texas," said Casey. "Lots of tornadoes and rattlesnakes there, you know. You might want to know, too, Sister Sarah, the military has an airstrip there where they train women pilots. Most people don't know that, though."

Sarah said, "Hmph." Then she asked Casey, "Oh, Casey, while you were taking a shower, John told me that you were picking peaches. How was it?"

"Well," answered Casey. "It was hard. Not like ah expected."

"Yeah. We did lots of that work when we were kids. All field work is hard. Many people don't know that unless they have worked out there," said Sarah.

"Aye," said Popeye. "We picked peaches, grapes, apricots, prunes, cotton, and chopped cotton. We picked melons and tomatoes near Huron, too. In the summer after school was out, we would go to Hollister to pick apricots. We did all that. As kids, we worked just like big people. But our father didn't let us keep any of the money. We worked for the family's needs and our school clothes. Our brother Robert wasn't too happy about that. Once, he said 'papa is like a communist.' But he said it when papa wasn't around."

Casey then began to tell Popeye and Sarah about his experience in the bar. "You know the bar on Fifth Street where they pick up workers?"

"Aye," said Popeye. "Our cousin Eva owns it. She and her husband Julio opened it in 1940 and they ran it together until he died of cancer in 1943. Then Eva took it over."

"Oh," said Casey. "She said that they call her Heavy Evie."

Sarah laughed and said, "Yes, that's what they call her and she's a tough lady when it comes to that bar, but she has to be in a business like that and that's all she has. But you know, she has a big heart and will do almost anything for anybody that needs help. Whenever any of the church groups need donations, Eva always gives something. When I teach Catechism at the Church, she sometimes helps me. She really loves children. She and Julio only had one son named James. Two years ago, he died in the war. He was killed in London during a bombing raid by the Germans. Eva hasn't gotten over him and probably never will. She pays him and Julio a visit at the cemetery every Sunday morning."

"Well," said Casey. "There was a fight, but she took care of those guys pretty quick. They should have stopped when she told them to. Ah know that ah shore wouldn't want to ever give 'er any trouble. The cops came, but they didn't even go in."

"Aye," laughed Popeye. "I don't think that *they* would even want to take her in if they ever had to. They know she can handle it when things get out of hand. But Eva wouldn't ever give the cops any trouble."

Then laughing, Popeye said, "You know, she should have been a cop herself."

"Well, we better get going Casey," said Popeye. "Sonny and Willie are going to wonder about where we are."

"Sonny? Is he back?" asked Sarah.

"Aye," answered Popeye. "He's back and he says he's going to be around to help Don Diego with his grapes this year."

"Good!" said Sarah. "He's a good and hard-working man and Don Diego and his family are really good people, too. I see them at mass every Sunday. John?"

"Aye, Sister, I'll try to go this Sunday," said Popeye before Sarah finished an anticipated lecture on his not going to Mass.

"Well, thank you very much, Sister Sarah," said Casey, as they began to leave. "It was a mighty good dinner."

"You are welcome, Casey," responded Sarah. "Please come again. Oh, John, please say hello to Sonny for me, and tell him and his friend Willie to come by soon. Maybe you can all come to dinner soon. I would like to meet Willie, too. I bet he's a real nice man."

"He's a boy of sixteen, Sister," said Popeye.

"What?" said Sarah. "What's he doing out here?"

"Being a hobo like the rest of us," said Casey. "He's a good and smart kid, and we're all going to take care of him."

With that, Popeye smiled to himself and started to feel better about Casey's attitude toward Willie.

As Popeye and Casey walked east from Sarah's house to the tracks, the day's heat was starting to feel less intense. As they passed some homes, children were out in some front yards playing and showering each other with hoses. The squeals and laughter sounded good to Popeye. He and Sarah and his other siblings had played like that many times when they were children. "Aye, to be a child again," sighed Popeye.

"Yeah," said Casey. "They just play all day and don't worry about anything until they have to go to school."

"Well," said Popeye. "Don't forget what we told you about kids having to work, too. These kids are probably home already after being in the fields all day with their moms and dads."

"Yeah, you're right Popeye. Ah forgot about that. But do they all work like that?"

"Aye," said Popeye. "Most of them do unless they are old enough to go downtown and sell newspapers like I did. That's the way life is around here. It's been that way ever since I can remember. But you know, it's a good life. Big families or little families, we have close family lives like the way it should be. I miss that part most of all when I think about being a child and about my life until now. We ate together, slept together in a small house, went to church together, and worked together. And we had fun together with a life lots of love. Aye, I have no complaints and no regrets."

As the two arrived at the tracks, they looked south where their campsite was. No one appeared to be there. On the other side of the fence, however, there was someone in the vineyard. As Casey and Popeye got closer, they could see that it was Don Diego. He was irrigating the grapevines. Don Diego looked up and saw the two walking up. He waved at them. They waved back and Casey called out, "Hello, Don Diego. Thanks again for the peaches."

"Okay," responded Don Diego. Then he asked, "Where's Sonny today?"

"He should be here pretty soon," answered Popeye and Casey at the same time.

"Okay," said Don Diego. "Tell him that my new grandson's name is Thomas."

"Thomas. Okay, we will tell him," said Casey.

Sonny and Willie arrived a short time later. They waved to Casey and Popeye as they got closer. Sonny spoke as he walked closer, "Well, Casey, were the peaches good to you today?"

"Well," answered Casey. "The peaches were okay. It was the heat, the fuzz, and the wasps that weren't."

Sonny looked at him, and asked, "Did you get stung, Casey?"

"Yeah, on mah hand. But Don Diego's cure for it worked good. But guess what? Ah got a couple of peaches for Willie." He handed the bag with the peaches to Willie.

"Oh," said Willie. "That's really kind of you, Mr. Casey. Thank you. Thank you."

"Well, Willie, ah figured that ah could at least do something for you since you helped me with my leg."

"Oh yes, sir, Mr. Casey. And we bought some more liniment because I thought that we would need it."

"Well, ah know that ah do," said Casey.

"Aye. Me, too," said Popeye.

"Me, too," joined Sonny.

Willie ate a peach first and commented how sweet it was. He had not had a piece of any fresh fruit since he left Kentucky. Today, it was not only a treat, it was a celebration for him. Then, he began massaging Casey's leg, then Popeye's, then Sonny's arms, and finally his own leg.

Evening was now arriving and the sun began to set to the west in a spectacularly bright red-orange curtain-like sheet of light. A flock of blackbirds flew over on their way home. In the distance, dogs barked and some of Don Diego's loose chickens chased each other noisily among the vines. The smell from the refinery filled the air as oil was being processed at the plant. Pipes hissing from the refinery's plant made an annoying noise at times. No trains could be heard and none were in sight, even though they would be bound from Fresno soon.

As the men sat down to just talk because they had all had dinner already, Sonny laid back against the dirt mound that supports the tracks.

Willie did the same and Casey and Popeye just sat on the ground. "Hey, Popeye," said Sonny. "Got any good stories tonight?"

"Aye, mate. How about the one about the ghost in the old house on Twelfth?"

"Okay, that sounds like a good one," responded Sonny.

Before telling a "made up" story, Popeye would always look up at the sky as if he was looking for God's permission to tell a big lie and not go to hell. He looked up, hesitated, and then he started, "Aye, mates. If there ever was a scary place, it was that big empty two-story house on Twelfth Avenue a few miles out of Hanford near a slough. Last year, a mate and I ran in there out of the rain one night. We decided to stay there after working at a ranch since it had been raining pretty hard and it didn't look like it was going to stop. We didn't have a ride and it was too far to walk home in that cold rain.

"We got inside through a busted door. We didn't have any light in there except for a small candle that we found and we lit the candle with some matches. But in about a minute, it went out. The other mate said he was afraid of the dark. I said to him, 'If you're afraid of the dark, then go outside.' But I was joking with him. Then in the dark he said, 'Hey, let go of my arm Popeye!' But I didn't touch him. I said, 'Hey, I'm over here and I didn't touch you, mate!' He said, 'Well, somebody did.' I told him that maybe somebody else was there so I called out, 'Anybody here?' There was no answer. Then I noticed that it had gotten colder in there. Then we heard footsteps upstairs. 'Hey,' I whispered. 'There must be somebody up there.' I said, 'Let's light a match and we can go see.' 'You go see!' the mate said. 'Okay,' I told him. 'And you can stay here alone in the dark and have someone touch you again.' The mate then said that he would go with me after all.

"We started going up the stairs where there was a little more light, then I found another candle and I lit it up. Then a man's face appeared at the top of the stairs. No body, hands, chest, or legs. Just a face. I said to myself, 'That face is uglier than mine!' 'Hello,' I said out loud. 'Did we wake you up?' The face just looked at us and then a chair came flying down the stairs at us. 'Hey!' I said, 'If you don't want us here, just say so.' Then a voice came out of the face and in a rough voice, it said, 'Get out!' Then my mate screamed. I turned around and he was holding onto his leg. I asked him what happened? 'I don't I know, but think a dog bit me because a heard a growl like a dog and saw some shiny eyes.' 'Let's get out of here, mate," I told him. We went to the door, but we couldn't open it. Then my mate screamed again. He was holding onto the other leg. I picked up a board and started swinging it around near the floor. Then we heard a growl and then I felt a bite on my leg. I just swung down by my leg and we heard a dog growl again. I turned around and kicked the door real hard and it opened. We ran out into the rain and kept running until we were far enough from the house. We didn't talk all the way home. When we got to my mate's house, he said, 'Next time, I'll walk in the rain.'"

"That *was* a spooky story, Mr. Popeye," said Willie. "I'm never going in any old empty houses."

"Well," said Casey. "Me, neither. But sometimes the lived in ones have some scary people, too." With that, they all burst out laughing.

Certainly, Popeye was a good storyteller, Sonny thought to himself. *But that wasn't his best.* He thought that he would soon ask Popeye to tell his famous whale story. That would have everybody on their edge.

After breakfast in the warm morning, Sonny, Popeye, and Willie went back to digging ditches. Casey decided that he wasn't going to let peach picking get the best of him, so he walked back to the bar on Fifth Street to catch a ride. Everyone could tell as they went to their jobs that this was going to be a hot day. *Another scorcher,* thought Sonny. *Maybe we ought to catch a ride with someone to the river to cool off.*

There were two spots that people would go to the Kings River for fun. One was next to what used to be Kingston near Laton, and another about eight miles north of Hanford going to Fresno. Many people, mostly families, would go there to cool off every summer, and sometimes it really got crowded. Sonny thought it would be a good trip to make on Sunday if the rest of the group wanted to go. He felt like he had a family now and he felt good about that. He didn't talk about any family and most people who knew him didn't ask about it. It was well known, however, that he loved children and especially enjoyed talking to them, especially the very young ones. Whenever he did go to the river, which was not often, he was always watching that no child got too far away from the bank or their parents.

That late afternoon, everyone came home tired. It was obvious that the heat, as well as the hard work, had taken its toll on all of them. The heat in the Valley was never a humid type. It was a dry heat and it exhausted people very quickly if they weren't careful. Drinking lots of water wasn't the only thing to do. Wearing hats, bandanas, and short-sleeved shirts were sometimes a must and not necessarily the style. Chickens walked around with beaks open and dogs lay in the shade with tongues hanging. Plants sometimes wilted in the heat if they hadn't been watered in the early morning. Some of the neglected outhouses would emit a stench that sometimes was unbearable. One could hear the "whirring" sound of evaporative coolers and condensers in cooling systems of stores. Cold soft drinks, ice cream, and beer were popular during this season, and stores sometimes could not keep up with the demand because there was already a shortage on many food items and ingredients used to make the concoctions.

That evening, Popeye decided to go to the "hobo jungle" "to see what was going on." He asked if anyone else wanted to go. Sonny, Casey, and Willie all said that they were just going to stay at the camp.

In the morning as the men woke up to ready to go to work, they noticed that Popeye was not there. Sonny wondered if he had found something interesting to do, or maybe he had bought some "juice" and couldn't make it back. Or hopefully, he stayed at Sarah's house. "Well," said Sonny. "We have to go to work. Maybe Popeye will be meeting us there."

Casey went to the bar to catch his ride to pick peaches, and Sonny and Willie went to their job digging ditches.

It was hot again and it was a long day because Popeye never showed up to work. As the day ended, Sonny and Willie decided to go to the "hobo jungle" to see if Popeye was there. They met up with four men there. Sonny asked, "Anybody seen Popeye?"

"The Sheriff took him last night," answered one of the men.

"What did he do?" asked Sonny.

"They said that he was reported by a mother that he exposed himself to some kids," said the man. "But it wasn't him. It was Bruto. Bruto was taking a pee behind the old depot and the kids were laughing at him. Then he turned around and acted like he was peeing at them. When he did that, a little girl got scared and ran home screaming and her mother called the law. Bruto hopped a freight and left Hanford after that happened and so they came looking for somebody to take."

Upon hearing that a terrible injustice had just taken over his good friend, Sonny became angry. "Popeye would never do something like that. He loves children. I wish that I could find Bruto and drag him to the jail myself."

"You know that they wouldn't listen to you anyway, Sonny," said one of the men.

"Yeah, you're right," said Sonny. "But this is wrong. So very wrong. Come on, Willie, we need to think and talk about what we can do about this."

As they were walking to the campsite, they met up with Casey coming from the opposite direction. Casey greeted them, "Hey, fellas. Did Popeye show up for work?"

"No," answered Sonny. "He's in jail for something that he didn't do and would never do." Sonny told Casey about what happened. They arrived at the campsite and settled down to think and talk about what they could do about their good friend's misfortune.

As the men were talking, Willie noticed that someone was coming along the tracks toward them. "Look! Someone's coming," he said.

"It looks like a woman," said Casey. Then he recognized who it was. "It's Sister Sarah!"

As she got close, the men could see that she looked like she had been crying. "Sister Sarah, what's wrong?" said Casey.

"Hello, Casey. Hello, Sonny." She looked at Willie and said hello to him, too. Then, with tears in her eyes, she told them the bad news, "A deputy came to my house this afternoon and told me that my brother John was stabbed to death this morning in the jail."

Sonny dropped to the ground on his knees in shock, Casey just stood there looking at Sarah in disbelief, and Willie started crying. Sarah then said, "I have to go now. God bless and watch over all of you."

Still in obvious deep shock, the men did not say anything.

As the day started to turn into evening, the three men still sat quietly and did not even eat dinner. They did not joke about anything or talk and share experiences about how their day went. Casey decided to take a walk, but he made it known that he wasn't going to the "hobo jungle."

As the evening turned darker, Sonny and Willie sat and looked up at the sky as if waiting for something to happen. Suddenly, something *did* happen. A lone bright shooting star went over them. Willie smiled and shouted, "Praise the lord! Go, Popeye, go!"

"Yeah," Sonny shouted, too. "Go, Popeye, go!"

In the morning, the men got up and went to work. It was a long day as they all had Popeye on their minds. They would miss him forever. Such a person is not easily forgotten. For Sonny, knowing somebody like Popeye and then losing him made his life that more difficult. He had memories, but it was not the same as hearing him tell one of his stories or having a conversation with him. Sonny wondered if he would have another friend like Popeye ever again.

That afternoon, the men returned to the campsite. Willie lay resting with his back on the railroad mound with his hands behind his back.

Then suddenly, Casey shouted, "Willie, there's a big spider on your arm!" But before Willie could shake it off, the spider bit him and he let out a loud moan in pain.

Sonny said, "Oh, no. It was a Black Widow." Then he jumped up and smashed it with a stick before it got away. Sonny didn't want to tell Willie then, but the Black Widow spider was the most poisonous spider in the area and probably the worst in the country.

Willie had felt a pain like lightning going up his arm where the spider had bit him. He sat there not knowing what to do. He had a face that showed pain in it, and his eyes were wide open and his eyeballs were bloodshot.

Sonny spoke up, "We need to get you to a doctor, but let's not move you now. I think it's better for you to be quiet and still. Casey, stay with Willie and I'll see about getting a doctor to come out here."

Sonny quickly left, almost running along the tracks. Casey looked at Willie. He was starting to sweat and he looked sick. Casey got up, sat next to Willie, and put his hand on his shoulder. "Don't worry little fella. We'll get help for you. You're going to be okay," he assured him.

"Mr. Casey, I'm scared. Maybe, I'm going to die," said Willie, with a frightened look on his face. "My grandma told me never to be afraid to die because Jesus would come to get me and take me to God. But right now, I'm real scared."

"Ya got to be quiet and stay still Willie," Casey told him. "Sonny said that ya got to."

Sonny was frantically going through town looking for any doctor offices that were open, but they were all closed. He stopped at the drugstore on Seventh Street to ask if anybody knew of any doctors who were available. One of the people at the drugstore told Sonny that he should go to the hospital to get help. Since Sonny didn't know where it was, he asked for directions. He realized that it was on the other side of town and that would lose him some valuable time to get there. Even then, he wondered if he could get anyone to go out to the tracks, and for a Negro at that. Many people looked at hobos as just "tramps" or "bums" and many were also racially prejudiced, so he was thinking about how he was going to get around that if he had trouble.

It was dark now. Back at the campsite, Willie appeared to have fallen asleep. Casey looked at his face and now wished that he learned something about curing someone for Black Widow bites. He felt helpless, and after thinking about what had happened to Popeye, started becoming worried that Sonny had run into some trouble. He then thought about going to Don Diego's house for help, but he did not want to leave Willie alone.

After about another hour went by, a train went by noisily and then it got very quiet. The sound of a dove cooing broke the still and quiet evening. In the moonlight, Casey looked at Willie's face. He did not seem to be breathing. Casey said to Willie, "Willie, wake up little fella. Sonny's on his way." Then he shook Willie lightly, but Willie did not wake up. Death has a certain unique chill and stillness to it that humans and animals can feel it when it comes. Casey now had no doubt. The little guy that he seemed to shun when he first met him and was now like a little brother to him was dead. He shook Willie harder and started to cry. "Willie, Willie, ya can't go now little fella! I just started to like ya."

It was now a very quiet and sad night for Casey. He sat and stared at the sky. Then suddenly, a bright shooting star streamed across the dark sky. Casey's face then had a big grin on it the size of Texas. "Praise the lord," he shouted. Go, Willie, go! Go, little fella! Ya made it!"

Sometimes we think that we know who and what we are, but when it comes to relationships among our human peers as brothers and sisters, our lives sometimes change. Our personalities can change for better or worse. It does not matter who or what we are, but it matters more that we live a good and righteous life every day like it was going to be our last.

Sonny returned to the campsite with another hobo who he knew named Jim and two people who he met at the hospital. They had come to take Willie back to the hospital in their car. Casey stood up and then told them all that it was too late. Sonny slowly went over and checked Willie. When he realized that Casey was right, he dropped down on his knees and then sat down. He started crying and sobbing, "God, he's just a child! He's just a child! This was no place for him to die."

Willie's body was taken away by the two people who came with Sonny. They had assured him that they would make sure to get him to the hospital. There, it would be decided where to take Willie's body for the arrangements for his burial.

Jim decided to stay the night with Sonny and Casey. He thought that losing two good friends in such a short time was too much for them, and so he would keep them company tonight.

Early in the morning, it was still dark as they slept. Sonny was suddenly awakened by a voice that sounded like Popeye. "You have to go, mate. They are coming for you!"

With that, Sonny hurriedly gathered his belongings and looked at Casey and Jim sleeping. He didn't wake them up, but he nodded to them. Then he left quietly but quickly, heading south along the tracks leading away from Hanford.

A rooster's crowing in the distance woke Casey and Jim in the brightly lit morning. Jim asked, "Hey, where's Sonny?"

Casey looked around. All of Sonny's belongings were gone. He then realized that Sonny didn't go off to work or just left for a walk. He was *gone*.

Jim then asked, "Do you think he'll be back? Will we see him again?"

"Yep," answered Casey confidently and with a smile. "We will see him again somewhere."

THE END

WHERE IS MY HOME?

Amy huddled closer to her mother. It was a cold and foggy January in 2009. The ground was damp, and so were Amy's clothes and hair. This morning there weren't any drum fires and no one else was around to start one.

Amy, nine years old, her mother Mary, and her little five-year-old brother Jamie had spent the night in the truck ramp at the rear of a large department store. It was the second night that they had spent the night here. Amy had heard her mother tell someone who had given them money in front of the store that they were going to a shelter. But that's not where they went. Instead, they went behind the store where they could hide from the police or anyone else who might turn them in. A homeless mother with children would certainly bring attention to them, and that could mean trouble.

Amy's mother was not well. She was very thin. She had been drinking heavily for the past two years. She was suffering from slight memory loss and malnutrition. This morning, she had been coughing, as she had been all night. She had also been a smoker. Her past bad habits, although relatively brief, were taking a toll on her.

Mary had lost her job as a cashier at a supermarket two years ago. The store had to close due to heavy loss in business because of the poor economy. She was not able to find another job, and her unemployment benefits had run out.

Jamie shivered and whimpered, "I'm hungry, momma."

"We'll go get something to eat soon, baby," his mother said in a hoarse and weak voice.

Usually, they could get handouts of money but they tried not be too obvious on the streets. But then, they might get lucky and find some discarded food in one of the dumpsters behind one of the nearby restaurants. It was always cold food, of course, but it was something to put in their stomachs, and maybe, for the rest of the day.

They heard a truck coming close. They jumped up and started gathering their few belongings. They exited the ramp in time to see a large truck drive up and then back up to the ramp. They saw the driver look back through one of the side-view mirrors. Apparently, he was being careful not to back up into someone asleep in the ramp.

The family walked away shivering and carrying their things in a shopping cart. Amy shoved her long, matted, stringy hair back and tugged down on her knitted cap as they walked. Her blue eyes were bright, but they had a faraway look in them.

As they walked, Amy thought about the day her father Hank Mulberry had come home and told her mother that he had lost his job at the auto dealership where he worked washing cars and doing odd jobs. The auto sales business had become very bad with the downturn in the economy. Hank's boss had to close down the business. Hank had enough trouble finding that job after he had been laid off at the cheese plant where he had worked for twelve years. It was something that Hank thought would never happen, because the dairy industry was doing very well during the time he worked there.

When she heard the bad news from Hank, Mary buried her face in her hands, and cried. "What are we gonna do now Hank? What are we gonna do now?"

Hank answered with uncertainty in his voice, "I'll find another job doing something."

"You're not the only one looking for a job out there, you know."

"I'll go see Jack at the junk yard. He might need some help."

"Jack?"

"Yes, Jack. Yeah, I know. He got busted for selling marijuana, but he's clean now and he's on probation, so he's not gonna take any chances."

"Yeah, that's what they all say."

Hank shrugged his shoulders, "I'll be back."

Hank went to the junkyard and found Jack cutting some metal with a blow torch. Jack stopped and pulled up the shield on his welding mask. "Hey, Hank! What's up?"

"Got any work for me, Jack? Pete had to close the business. Cars weren't selling."

Jack looked at him as if pondering for an answer. He shook his head, "Sorry, Hank. I'm just keeping up here myself. I shoulda gone into the recycling business. With so many folks trying to make ends meet, they're collecting cans and bottles and everything they can sell these days. And instead of junking their cars, people are keeping them and fixin' 'em up."

"But know what, Hank?" Jack looked around. "I know a guy who's always looking for guys to sell some weed. Interested?"

Hank looked at him. "Nah, I don't know Jack. I've never done anything like that before. Not even touched the stuff ever. Never been in any trouble before, and I don't want to get into any now."

"Hey, Hank, the way things are now, and I really think it's gonna get worse, a man's gotta do what he has to."

"Yeah, well, I don't think I'm that desperate yet."

Hank went home. Mary met him at the door. "Well, any luck Hank?"

"No, nothin' yet. I'll go out again tomorrow."

"Well, the rent's due Wednesday and we can't be late again."

"I'll go to the employment office tomorrow and sign up for unemployment and then go see about food stamps. Maybe we can get some help with the rent, too." Hank sounded unsure and tired.

As Amy listened to her parents talking, she began to get frightened because she really didn't understand what was happening. All she knew was that her parents seemed pretty worried, and now she was starting to feel it, too.

Hank went out every day for the next few days. Nothing was available. He didn't have much luck with unemployment or food stamps, either. Because of so many other people also out of work and needing assistance, his applications were taking too long to process and he was getting desperate. The rent was overdue and the family received a notice that the rent would have to be paid soon or they would be evicted.

Hank had always been a man of honesty and hard work. Now, however, his family's welfare was seriously being threatened. He had to do something, so he headed to Jack's.

As he walked in that cold morning, Hank started talking to himself in a low tone, *How did this happen? What did I do for things to get like this?*

Is God punishing me? Hank had no answers. He couldn't seem to think straight. He felt powerless.

Hank had been raised a Catholic but quit going to church when everything went bad. Now whenever he passed the church, he would mumble defiantly to himself, *Where are you now, God?* He briefly thought about the days when he and his wife would take the family to church. That's when everything was good.

He approached Jack's junkyard and stood there for a moment. He shook his head and started to turn around and head for home. Then he stopped and thought to himself, *If, at anytime, I needed to do something like this, it's now.*

Hank hurried into Jack's shop before he changed his mind. "Jack," he said in a low tone. "How do I get hold of that guy?"

Hank felt scared. He had just picked up two plastic bags of marijuana from someone he didn't even know except for the name Ro. Ro had called Jack and had asked if Hank was "okay." After "clearing" him, Ro instructed Hank what he had to do and to watch who he sold to, then sent him out.

Hank knew some people who used marijuana, although he didn't smoke it himself. He planned on making some contacts the next day, because it was getting late and he wasn't very anxious to get involved in any illegal work anyway. He stuffed the bags of marijuana in the pockets of his coat.

When he got home, Mary was cooking in the kitchen. She called out to him, "Hank, could you take out the bag of garbage on the porch? I don't want any cats to get it."

Hank said, "Okay." He put his coat on a chair and went out to the porch.

While Hank was outside taking out the garbage bag, Jamie grabbed his daddy's coat to look in the pockets. Sometimes, Hank would stop at a store and get some candy for the kids, but this time he didn't. Jaime found the bags with marijuana. "Momma, what's this?" he asked, as he took the bags to his mother. Mary took one look and immediately knew what it was. "Oh, no!" She grabbed the bags from Jaime, opened them, dumped the marijuana in the sink, and ran the water flushing it down the drain.

As Hank walked through the door, Mary screamed at him, "Hank, are you crazy? Do you wanna go to jail?"

"What are you talking about? Calm down!"

"Calm down? You know what I'm talking about. Those bags in your coat!"

Hank grabbed his coat and felt inside the pockets. Hank's face turned pale, then red with anger. "Wh-what did you do with the bags, Mary?" he demanded.

"I flushed that dope down the drain Hank! What on earth were you thinking?"

"No!" screamed Hank, grabbing his hair. "That was five hundred dollars' worth of stuff. That guy's gonna kill me now!"

Mary buried her face in her hands, and cried. She sobbed, "My God, Hank. Why did you do this? Why on earth is this happening to us?" Then she looked up. "What now, Hank? What now?"

"I gotta leave, that's what!"

Hank was scared. Amy and Jamie heard everything and started to cry. The children didn't understand everything, but they knew that their parents were arguing and this was not good.

Hank grabbed his coat, went out the door in the cold, and didn't come back. That was the last time that Amy had seen her father

Mary waited up all night for Hank to return. She fell asleep on the couch and woke up there in the morning. She thought that maybe he would be coming through the door any minute, but he never came.

Two days went by and Hank didn't return. While the children went to school, Mary decided to go to Jack's. Maybe Hank would be there. But when she got there, there was no Hank. She saw Jack welding and approached him. "Jack. Jack, has Hank been here?"

Jack pulled up his welding mask. He looked at her with a surprised look on his face. "Hello, Mary. No, Hank hasn't been here. I haven't seen him since the day before yesterday."

Mary, crying, began to tell Jack what had happened. As she told him how Hank just walked out the door and hasn't been back, she couldn't help saying it, "It's your fault, Jack. You put him up to this."

Jack listened and shook his head, "Oh, no! Listen, Mary, I was just trying to help. Things are really bad right now. He told me how desperate he was to provide for his family. But why did you have to flush the stuff done the drain? That guy Ro is gonna be after Hank to pay him for the stuff. That's why he left."

Mary, crying again, screamed at Jack, "It's your fault and I'll report you to the police!"

"Please, don't do that Mary. That'll just make things worse. Let me talk to Ro and see if I can reason with him. Just go home and I'll let you know what happens."

Later that morning, Jack went to Mary's house. She heard him knock. She went out to the porch to meet him. "Well, what happened?" Mary asked impatiently and looked at Jack for some sign of relief.

"I tried talking to Ro, Mary, but he wants the five hundred dollars. He wants it by noon tomorrow. If he doesn't get it, he's sending somebody out here. I'm sorry."

Mary looked at Jack with a horrified look. "He's coming here? For what? I don't have any money! Maybe I should just call the police."

"Please don't, Mary. Look, I have $50. That's all I can spare. Why don't you take it and get yourself and the kids on a bus right away and go to some relative or friend out of town for a while. Maybe Ro will forget about you."

Mary snatched the money from Jack's hand. "Get outta here, Jack, before I call the police on you. You brought this on us by your real smart advice to Hank. Now I have to take my kids and hide? I hope you burn in hell, Jack!"

Mary went to the school where Amy and Jamie attended and got them out by telling the vice-principal that there was a family emergency. Nothing could be further from the truth. A gangster or who knows what was now going to be looking for them, and they had to get out of town as quickly as possible.

Mary got the kids home and made a fast meal with whatever was in the refrigerator. She was trying to use up what food they could not take with them. She got out what food they could take and put in it plastic bags.

Amy asked her mother, "Are we going to look for daddy, momma?"

Mary hesitated to think about her response before she answered. She thought it best to tell the kids the truth. "No, we're not going to look for daddy because I don't have any idea where he is. We have to leave here because a bad man might be looking for us. But I will take care of you, so don't worry. We can't tell anybody where we're going or why. Okay?"

"Okay, momma. But can you tell us where were going?"

"Right now, I don't know, baby. We're just going to leave, okay? Pack as much clothes as you can in these bags and help Jamie do the same. Don't take anything that you might not need, but make sure that you take warm clothes and a blanket. Pack a few toys for Jamie and take some of your books, too."

Mary called her friend Janice. "Janice, sorry to bother you, but I have a serious problem and I need to get me and my kids out of town. Could you come over and give us a ride right away? I have gas money."

The family took what they could and walked out the door. They were not to ever return to the house. Janice drove Mary and her children forty miles away to another town, and just dropped them off at a public park as Mary had asked her to. From there and for almost a year now, they wandered and spent days and nights behind stores and shopping malls.

"Amy? Amy, honey." Amy didn't hear her mother at first when she was thinking about the days that led up to their present situation. "What, momma? I'm sorry, I didn't hear you."

"Are you okay, honey?"

"Yes, momma, I was just thinking."

"Thinking about what, honey?"

"Oh, just thinking about us and daddy. I miss school, too, momma."

As they walked, Mary glanced over at Amy and felt angry and sad at the same time. Here she was in the street with her children. Not only did they not have a warm house to live in, but they were also missing out on their education and friends.

Then she thought about Hank. *Where could he be? Did he ever return to the house?* She hoped not. Since she couldn't and wouldn't dare tell anyone where they went to, it would be hard for him to find them.

Mary decided that this morning they would check a dumpster behind a restaurant that served breakfast. She thought that they might be throwing out food that probably wasn't too cold. As they went behind the restaurant, Mary looked to see if anyone was around. Then as they approached the dumpster, a large older man came out the back door of the restaurant carrying a large pan with left-over food. He saw Mary and the children. Then with an angry look on his face, he demanded, "What are you doing there?"

"My children are hungry and just I wanted to get them something to eat, sir."

"Stealing, that's what you was up to. Wasn't you? There ain't nothin' there for you. A guy'll come around later and take it for his pigs. Are you pigs?"

"No, sir."

"Well, you look like pigs! Look at you! You should be ashamed of yourself! Why don't you get a job? Where's your old man? Is he in jail? I should call the cops and have 'em haul you and your little snots away for being dirty bums!"

"Oh, no! Please don't, sir. We'll leave," Mary pleaded.

"You better believe you're gonna leave." With that, he grabbed an old pipe off the ground and slammed it on the side of the dumpster, making a loud bang. Amy screamed and Jamie started to cry. Mary felt her heart beating fast and quickly walked away with her arms tightly wrapped around their shoulders. She said to them with assurance, "Don't be scared. He's just a mean old man. He doesn't know any better. We have to ask God to forgive him."

The man laughed at them out loud, "Look at 'em, running like scared rabbits!"

Amy couldn't help feeling scared and ashamed. That mean old man made her feel like she was really doing something terrible. She wondered what her friends would think if they saw her like this. The tears started to stream down her face as she wept silently. Then, she couldn't help herself. She started shaking uncontrollably, and crying, "Oh, daddy, where are you?"

At that moment, Mary realized that this ordeal had taken Amy over the edge. She stopped walking, grabbed Amy, and hugged her tightly. Then she also began shaking and weeping. Jamie joined in, and the three stood there hugging and crying together.

When they quieted down, Mary told the children, "Enough of this! We're going to a shelter."

Jamie spoke, something he didn't do very often, "What's a shelter, momma?"

Amy, feeling better and happy at hearing her mother's good news, felt it her duty to tell her little brother what it meant. "It's a place where we'll have real beds to sleep in and real food to eat like at home, Jamie."

"You think we'll find some friends there, Amy?" Jamie asked with a smile that that was as bright as the sun that was now starting to show through the slowly lifting fog.

Amy thought for a second, then she answered her little brother with her arm around him, "I'm sure we will, Jamie. Not everybody's mean." Then swallowing hard, she added, "And not everybody thinks we're pigs either."

Jamie looked at her and started grunting and making sounds like a pig. They all burst out laughing.

It wasn't often that Jamie made anyone laugh, so Mary felt that somehow this was going to help change him for the best. She had been very worried about him. Jamie had been seeing the psychologist at the school where the children attended. Although a bright child, Jamie had started being very shy and sometimes withdrawn during class activities. Then when he started crying in class at times for no apparent reason, they agreed to have the psychologist work with him. This had started after they began having financial problems.

As they walked toward the central area of the city, they looked around to see if there was anyone around that could maybe provide them with directions to a family shelter. She asked the children to "keep an eye out" for anyone that might look friendly.

Jamie spoke up, "Momma, why don't we wait at a bus stop? We could ask a bus driver where the shelter is."

"Why, that's a good idea, baby!"

Jamie smiled at his mother. His smile made her feel good.

They walked up to a bus stop, plastic bags and all, and waited. A woman walked up to wait for the bus. She looked at them, and immediately, a disgusted look showed on her face. She stepped back and stood in a spot a short distance away.

Mary noticed the woman's reaction to their presence, and looked at Amy and Jamie. She whispered to them, "It's okay."

A city bus roared up and then stopped with a creaking and hissing sound of the brakes. The door opened out with a hiss. The driver, a slender lady with stringy blonde hair showing under her driver's cap, peered out from her seat. With a deep and loud voice, she announced, "This is Route 15. Are you all gettin' on?"

Mary let the lady go first. She climbed up the steps and boarded the bus holding her nose. Mary ignored her, and asked the driver, "Does this bus go by any family shelters, ma'am?"

"Sure does, hon. You and the kids get on. I'll take you there. Need any help with your things?"

"Well, how much is it? I want to know if I have enough money." Mary had never ridden a city bus and so she had no idea what the fare would be.

The bus driver looked back in her rear-view mirror where she could see the few passengers on board. Then she leaned over, winked, and whispered to Mary, "A quarter each, hon. That's all. It ain't that far."

Mary said, "Okay. Come on, children. Get the bags on quickly."

The driver smiled at the kids and told them to put their bags on the floor next to her seat since their stop would be second. As they boarded, she swallowed hard as she saw the condition of their worn and soiled clothes and their long and tangled hair. She felt a warm flutter in her heart, and with a watery sensation in her eyes, whispered softly to herself, "God bless'm and help'm."

Without being noticed, the driver wiped her eyes and then introduced herself, "Muh name's Millie. Why don't you set up front here since your stop is second on the route?" She thought that if she had sent them to further back, the other passengers would probably complain and the family would feel hurt if they made rude remarks. After all, they had been out on the streets for a long time and they needed bathing and their clothes needed washing.

The bus traveled a few blocks and came to the first route stop. Two people got up and came to the front where the opened door awaited them. As they passed by where Mary and the children sat, one of them blurted in a low voice, "How disgusting!"

Millie said, "Have a good day, folks!" Then when the door closed, she said, "Ya lousy excuse for a person!"

Mary looked at Millie and smiled, "I'm sure she didn't hear you."

"I couldn't care less, hon. There are some people that I just tolerate, but if I had my way . . ." she made a fist and shook it with a threatening gesture.

Mary decided that she liked Millie. Maybe she was somebody she could trust. She hesitated because she didn't want to appear nosey, then she asked Millie, "Do you have a family, Millie?"

"Nope. Not really. It's just me. You see, I live at the shelter. I just got this job, but I'm going to be getting my own place soon. The people at the shelter said I could stay there until I got a job and have enough money to rent someplace decent."

Mary was impressed. Not only did Millie seem to be a caring person, but she was also a homeless person like herself and her children. No wonder she was so kind and friendly. Now it was clear to Mary why Millie didn't like those arrogant people that had made rude and mean remarks about them. Millie's own actions and comments about those people were probably a reflection of what she had been through, and now she was probably sort of reliving it.

The next stop was where Mary and her children were to get off. Millie announced that it was the second stop. Two people got up to leave. This time, however, no one said anything about Mary and her children. One of them just said to Millie, "See you tomorrow, Millie."

Millie responded, "Okay, John. See you tomorrow. Take care."

Mary asked, "Is this where we get off, Millie?"

"Yes, it is, hon. The shelter is that building we just passed. It's the white one with the red roof."

"Oh, okay I see it. Come on, children. This where we get off."

Amy and Jamie got up quickly and grabbed their bags. Mary and Millie looked at each other and smiled. They knew that the children were excited.

Millie said to Mary, "See ya tonight, Mary. We'll have time to talk at dinner after prayers."

"That'll be great, Millie."

"Yeah, we'll have a great time. And listen, tell Marge that I'll be off early tonight after all, so I'll be able to help in the kitchen. We all help out, you know. Maybe you'll work in the kitchen, too, after you get settled."

"I'd happy to and maybe the children can help, too."

"Oh, yeah, there's always something for everybody to do."

Mary and the children walked to the shelter and Mary felt a little nervous. She didn't know what to expect, but she was thinking about the children more than ever and she had to do what was best for them.

As the family walked into the shelter, a woman came out and greeted them. "Hello, my name is Margaret, but some people call me 'Large Marge' around here. I could never figure that out," she said, winking. Marge was a large heavy woman, so it was Mary's impression that Marge had a real sense of humor.

Marge smiled and said, "Well, I guess you're looking for someplace to stay huh?"

Mary smiled and said, "Yes, ma'am. We've been out on the street for almost a year now, and I thought it was best we looked for something better, especially for the children. They haven't had a decent place to sleep or decent food eat for all this time. Uh, we had some problems and we had to—"

Marge stopped Mary and put her arm around her. "Don't worry, honey. We don't ask a lot of questions here. I'm in charge here and the only thing I ask is if you're here for the night or for a longer time. You're welcome to stay as long as you like or need to. Nobody here is going to tell you to leave unless you cause trouble, and you don't look like that kind."

"No, we're not troublemakers and we'll do our part around here, Marge. Millie told us everybody helps out. Oh, by the way, she said to tell you she'll be off early tonight to help in the kitchen."

"Good. Millie's real decent people, as you probably already found that out."

"Yes, ma'am. She's a real good lady."

"Well, welcome uh . . ."

"Oh, I'm sorry. My name's Mary. Mary Mulberry, and this is Amy and Jamie."

"Well, welcome Mulberry family! I sure you'll be happy here. Come on. I'll show you where your beds will be."

As Mary and the children followed, Marge suddenly stopped, and said, "Say, there's a gentleman here by the last name of Mulberry. Hank Mulberry is his name. Any relation?"

Mary froze. "Hank Mulberry is my husband's name! Is he here?"

"No, he's working. He just got a job at the carwash a few blocks from here."

"It's gotta be daddy!" Amy exclaimed with excitement in her voice.

Mary quickly told her, "Don't get too excited, honey. It might not be him."

At that point, Mary didn't know what to think. *If it was him, what was he doing out here and how would he react when he saw them?*

Mary described Hank to Marge. She responded with, "Yep, that's him. He should be comin' in pretty soon. I should get you and the kids settled and then you can wait to see if it's him for sure."

"Okay, Marge, we'll do that."

Marge showed Mary and the children where their beds and bathrooms were. She then took them by the kitchen and dining area. "This is where our whole family gets together for supper. Nothing like a good hot meal at the end of the day," she said. "And tonight, we're having fresh-baked apple pie and ice cream for dessert." She winked at Amy and Jamie as their eyes got big.

Mary and the children got settled, took hot baths, and changed to clean clothes. Then they sat on their beds waiting to see if it was Hank who would be coming through the door. Mary thought she would have a lot of questions for Hank and even started to get angry at him for leaving them. But then she decided that she should just be happy to see him and that he was alright. For the first time in more than two years, she closed her eyes and prayed, *Please God, let it be our Hank. Give us your blessing with a new start with our family being together again.*

Hank finally came through the door and walked down the hallway. Mary spotted him first as he started to pass the doorway to their room. He looked tired and older. But it was him and it looked like he was alright. Then she called out to him, "Hank!"

Hank looked at Mary and then at the children in disbelief. Tears filled his eyes. Mary and the children got up and ran to him. Hank hugging them and sobbing said, "Thank you God! I've been looking for you. Janice told me she dropped you off at a park here and I looked everywhere. Where have you been?"

At dinner and after many prayers of thanks, Hank told Mary how he had come to the shelter looking for them, stayed there, and then found the job at the carwash. He had contacted Jack who had worked out a repayment plan for him with Ro.

"Now, thank God, we're together again," said Hank with his arms tightly around his family. "We'll make it, Mary. We'll make it."

Amy looked at her parents with teary eyes and a smile and thought, *we will make it, daddy, we will. Thanks to God!*

THE END

www.ingramcontent.com/pod-product-compliance
Lightning Source LLC
Chambersburg PA
CBHW022231080526
44577CB00005B/88